Love, Trust & Leather

A Guide to Mastering the Art of BDSM Punishments

Clare Hill

Anderson Hill

Published by Clare Hill and Anderson Hill

First published in 2024 in Perth, Australia.

Copyright © Clare Hill and Anderson Hill

All rights reserved. No part of this publication may be reproduced, stored in a retrieval system or transmitted in any form or by any means, electronic, mechanical, photocopying, recording or otherwise, without the prior permission of the publisher.

All inquiries should be made to the authors.

For Those Who've Moved Beyond Fuzzy Handcuffs

Contents

Welcome to the World of Advanced BDSM Punishments — vii
Preparing for Punishment Setting the Stage for Success — xv

1. The Whisper Challenge – Words They'll Never Forget — 1
2. The Countdown Confession – Tick-Tock and Talk — 6
3. Ordeal Tasks – Where Discipline Meets Evil Genius — 10
4. Impact Play – When Words Aren't Enough — 15
5. Sensory Deprivation – Silence is Golden — 20
6. Chastity as Punishment – Lock It Down — 25
7. Writing Assignments – Words of Regret — 30
8. Public Embarrassment – Subtle Thrills in the Real World — 33
9. The Gag Challenge – Silence Is Punishment — 37
10. Tickling Torment – Laugh Till You Obey — 41
11. Overstimulation – When Enough Isn't Enough — 45
12. Denial and Edging – So Close, Yet So Far — 50
13. Temperature Play – The Heat of the Moment (and the Chill of Control) — 54
14. The Clothing Rule – Dressing for Discipline — 58
15. Corner Time with a Twist – The Art of Doing Nothing — 62
16. Ice Play with a Punishing Twist — 66
17. Forced Stillness – The Unmoving Ordeal — 71
18. The Humiliation Box – A Lesson in Vulnerability — 75
19. Weighted Patience – Bearing the Burden — 78
20. Obstacle Crawl – Earning Forgiveness — 83

21. Sensory Chaos – The Overload Ordeal	87
22. Controlled Bruising – Marking the Moment	91
23. Role Reversal – The Switch Punishment	95
24. The Silent Countdown – A Game of Anticipation	99
The Final Lesson – Dominance, Submission, and the Art of Connection	103
Clare and Anderson An Evening to Remember	107
About the Author	111

Welcome to the World of Advanced BDSM Punishments

Let's be honest—punishment in BDSM is one of the most electrifying parts of the dynamic. It's where the rules meet creativity, the serious meets the playful, and the power exchange really takes center stage. But here's the thing—good punishment? It's not just about dishing out orders or swinging a paddle like it's a magic wand. No, it's about connection. It's about understanding each other so well that every scene feels intimate, personal, and, let's be honest, unforgettable.

We're Anderson and Clare, and we know how messy—and wonderful—this can get. Anderson's days are consumed by high-powered meetings and demanding decisions, while Clare's world revolves around precise schedules and endless deadlines. But when the workday ends, our focus shifts completely to each other, creating a space where trust and creativity take center stage. One night, after Clare forgot (for the third time!) to put the toys back in the drawer, I decided to do something a little different. I handed her my favorite hardcover book and said, "Balance this on your head. Now, recite Shakespeare. Perfectly."

It started as a bit of a joke—both of us were laughing as she wobbled through "To be or not to be." But then something happened. That moment turned into this intense, vulnerable experience. I watched her push herself—not out of fear, but because she genuinely wanted to meet my expectations. And for me? It hit me how much trust and intention goes into surrender. It wasn't just about the book. It was about us.

And that's why we're here, writing this book. Because punishment, when it's done right, is so much more than a slap on the wrist or a time-out. It's an experience. It's a shared moment of trust, playfulness, and power. And whether it's deeply intense or laugh-out-loud ridiculous, it's the stuff that makes your dynamic uniquely yours.

An Invitation to the Experienced

In the world of BDSM, punishment is far more than a consequence. It's an art—a dance of power, vulnerability, and connection. This book isn't for beginners dabbling with cuffs for the first time or unsure where to begin. No, this is for the Dominants who've mastered the basics, for the submissives who crave a deeper understanding of their role, and for those partnerships ready to elevate their dynamic to breathtaking new heights.

Here, punishment isn't simply about correction or control. It's about trust, pushing boundaries, and exploring the depths of your shared desires. Through 20 techniques, we invite you to embrace creativity, precision, and purpose as you hone the skills that make BDSM a profound and unforgettable experience.

Why Punishment Matters

To outsiders, the concept of punishment might seem harsh or even cruel. For those within the BDSM community, however, it's something else entirely. Punishment is an act of care and guidance. It's a tool to enforce boundaries, reinforce roles, and remind both Dominant and submissive of the beautiful dynamic they've built together.

Punishment can be many things: a firm hand to correct behavior, a playful tease to enforce obedience, or an elaborate ordeal that tests patience and trust. It's never about mindless cruelty; it's about purpose, connection, and, most importantly, consent.

For the Dominant, the punishment offers an outlet to express authority, creativity, and care. It's a chance to refine your techniques, test your partner's limits, and deepen the bond you share.

For the Submissive, the punishment is an opportunity to show devotion, embrace vulnerability, and find empowerment within the structure of the dynamic.

Each punishment you'll explore in this book is more than an act—it's a shared experience, carefully designed to enhance your dynamic and leave a lasting impression.

Consent

Let's start with the most critical foundation: consent.

In BDSM, consent isn't a simple yes or no. It's a nuanced, ongoing agreement that ensures both parties feel safe, respected, and enthusiastic about what's to come. Every punishment described in this book is built on the principle that consent is sacred.

Before engaging in any form of punishment, communication is key. Discuss:

- Boundaries - What's off-limits?
- Triggers - Are there physical or emotional areas to avoid?

- Safe Words - Agree on clear signals to pause or stop the scene if needed.

Even if you've been with your partner for years, never skip the negotiation phase. Dynamics evolve, limits shift, and ensuring consent is a sign of respect and care.

Negotiation

Negotiation is where fantasy becomes reality. It's where you take your partner's desires, fears, and curiosities and craft them into a scene that's as safe as it is electrifying. How to Negotiate:

Talk First, Play Later

Outline the scene beforehand. This isn't the time to wing it or assume you know what your partner wants or needs. Sit down together in a neutral, relaxed environment and discuss your ideas openly. What are you hoping to achieve with this scene? Is the focus on correction, trust-building, or pushing boundaries? For example, if you're planning a punishment, talk about the details:

- What kind of tools will be used?
- What intensity is desired?
- Are there any areas of the body that should be avoided?
- What emotional reactions might arise, and how should they be handled?

By talking first, you're setting the stage for success. This also gives both of you the opportunity to clarify expectations and ensure there's no room for misunderstandings once the scene begins. It's not just practical—it's a crucial step in creating excitement and anticipation for what's to come.

Be Specific

Vagueness can lead to confusion, frustration, or even accidental boundary-crossing. Saying "I'll punish you" may sound enticing in theory, but in practice, it leaves too many unanswered questions. Specificity is your best friend in negotiation. Instead, spell out the details clearly:

- "You'll receive 10 strikes with a paddle on your thighs."
- "You'll kneel for 15 minutes in the corner with your hands behind your head."
- "I'll tie your hands with silk restraints and blindfold you before using the flogger."

This clarity ensures that both partners know what to expect and can give informed consent. It also helps avoid situations where one person might interpret "punishment" differently from the other. Specificity doesn't ruin spontaneity—it enhances it by removing uncertainty and allowing both parties to fully immerse themselves in the scene without hesitation.

Mutual Agreement

Remember, a submissive's submission is a gift—not a guarantee. Just because they've agreed to a D/s dynamic doesn't mean every idea you propose will be accepted without discussion. Negotiation is a two-way street, where both Dominant and submissive have equal input into what will or won't happen.

For instance, if a Dominant suggests corner time followed by spanking, the submissive might say, "I'm okay with the spanking, but standing in the corner triggers bad memories for me." A good Dominant listens, adjusts the plan, and ensures the submissive feels safe and respected. Here's what mutual agreement looks like:

- Both parties actively contribute to the negotiation process.
- Concerns or hesitations are addressed without judgment or pressure.
- Both agree on the safe word(s) and signals before proceeding.

Mutual agreement also means revisiting the terms of your dynamic regularly. Limits can change over time, and what feels exciting today might not feel the same tomorrow. Respecting your partner's autonomy and boundaries ensures the experience remains consensual, fulfilling, and built on trust.

Safety First: SSC and RACK

Safety is the unshakable backbone of BDSM. This book incorporates two widely respected frameworks to ensure your scenes are as thrilling as they are secure:

- SSC (Safe, Sane, and Consensual). Play should always be physically safe, mentally sound, and mutually agreed upon.
- RACK (Risk-Aware Consensual Kink). For those who love walking the razor's edge, RACK acknowledges that some activities carry inherent risks. The key is being fully informed and prepared for those risks before you dive in.

Whether you lean toward SSC or RACK, remember: Preparation and vigilance are non-negotiable. Punishment is only fun when it's safe.

The Psychology of Punishment

Punishment in BDSM isn't just physical—it's deeply psychological. To wield it effectively, you must understand the mindsets at play.

Understanding the Submissive Mindset

Submission isn't weakness; it's strength. A submissive offers their trust, their body, and their vulnerability, knowing their Dominant will cherish and respect those gifts. Punishment, in this context, becomes a reaffirmation of their role and the dynamic they've chosen.

Why Punishment Works? A well-executed punishment reinforces the structure of the relationship, allowing the submissive to feel secure within the boundaries set by their Dominant.

Aftercare is The Final Act of Trust

Aftercare is where everything comes full circle. No matter how intense the punishment or how wild the scene, this is the moment that cements the connection, ensuring both of you walk away feeling fulfilled, grounded, and closer than ever.

For the submissive, aftercare is a balm for body and soul. A soft blanket, a soothing touch, or whispered words of reassurance can help them process the raw physical and emotional intensity of the experience. It's the embrace that says, *You're safe, you're cherished, and I'm here.*

But let's not forget the Dominant. Yes, you need aftercare too. The rush of control, the mental focus, the weight of responsibility—it all takes its toll. Take a moment to breathe, reflect, and recharge. A glass of water, a quiet cuddle, or even a few minutes of silence can do wonders to help you decompress.

Skipping aftercare? That's like walking offstage without taking a bow, leaving the most important part of the story unfinished. This is the final act of trust, the soft landing after the storm, and the promise that whatever just unfolded was done with care, respect, and love. Don't miss it—it's

A Journey Worth Taking

This book isn't just a guide—it's a companion for those who are ready to embrace the complexity, creativity, and joy of advanced BDSM punishments. Each technique you'll explore is designed to challenge, inspire, and strengthen your dynamic, one carefully crafted scene at a time.

Ready to level up? Let's dive in and make punishment an art form—and maybe even have a little fun while we're at it.

Preparing for Punishment Setting the Stage for Success

Before you can wield that paddle like a virtuoso or tie a knot that would make a sailor jealous, you need to master the fine art of preparation. This isn't just about grabbing a toy and hoping for the best. No, preparation is where the magic starts. Think of this chapter as your pre-flight checklist: tools, communication, and groundwork to ensure every punishment is as smooth, safe, and satisfying as silk restraints. Let's be clear—punishment isn't something you "wing." Imagine trying to improvise a punishment scene and realizing halfway through that the paddle is in the other room, the rope is tangled in your headphones, and the dog is staring at you like, "Seriously?" Preparation isn't just practical—it's sexy. It sets the tone, builds anticipation, and ensures both of you are ready to dive into something unforgettable.

Tools, Toys, and Equipment Checklist

The Must-Haves

Every Dominant needs a toolkit, and no, we don't mean the

Preparing for Punishment Setting the Stage for Success

one in the garage. These aren't just objects; they're extensions of your creativity and authority. Think of them as the paintbrushes to your masterpiece—or the whisks to your kinky soufflé.

- Impact Play Tools: Floggers, paddles, canes, and, of course, your hands. Nothing beats the sound of a perfectly delivered smack echoing in the room.
- Restraints: Cuffs, ropes, or bondage tape. *Pro tip*: Keep scissors handy for emergencies. (Because while "stuck in restraints" sounds fun in theory, it loses its charm at hour three.)
- Blindfolds: A simple way to heighten anticipation and vulnerability. Bonus: they can't see you sneakily checking your notes.
- Vibrators and Other Toys: Perfect for blending pleasure with punishment. There's nothing like a good edge to keep them squirming.
- Temperature Play Items: Massage candles, ice cubes, or warming oils. Hot and cold sensations are your best friends here.
- Gags: Ball gags, bit gags, or even a silk scarf. Silence is golden, and a little drool is just a bonus.

The Nice-to-Haves

Ready to take it up a notch? These additions will add flair and versatility to your scenes:

- Furniture: Spanking benches, St. Andrew's crosses, or a sturdy chair. (Sturdy is the keyword here—flimsy IKEA chairs are not your friend.)
- Sensory Tools: Feathers, pinwheels, or brushes to tease and torment. Who knew craft-store finds could make someone shiver?

- Remote-Controlled Toys: Perfect for hands-free fun —or public mischief, if you're feeling daring.

Creating a Safe and Consensual Environment

Your environment isn't just a passive setting—it's an integral part of the experience. Whether you're transforming a bedroom into a seductive retreat or unveiling a fully equipped dungeon, the ambiance sets the tone for everything that follows. Privacy is essential; nothing disrupts the mood faster than an unexpected knock at the door, so make sure the space is secure and interruption-proof. Cleanliness is equally crucial, especially when toys are part of the play. A dusty paddle or sticky chair doesn't exactly inspire desire, so maintain hygiene to ensure comfort and safety. Organization also plays a pivotal role. Keep all essentials within reach; no one wants to ruin the rhythm of a scene by scrambling to find a misplaced flogger. Once the practical elements are in place, it's time to finesse the atmosphere. Lighting can transform a space—soft, dim lights add drama, while a red bulb heightens the heat and intensity. Music provides a powerful backdrop, whether it's sultry jazz, driving beats, or the simplicity of silence. Scent completes the sensory experience; candles, essential oils, or incense can evoke the desired mood. Choose fragrances like lavender, vanilla, or even leather to complement the theme and create a truly immersive environment.

Communicating Boundaries and Safe Words

Communication isn't just a nice-to-have—it's absolutely essential. Before introducing a paddle or setting the stage, sit down and talk. Far from being a "mood-killer," this conversation lays the foundation for the scene itself. Start by discussing hard limits—those absolute no-go areas that must be respected without exception. Treat these boundaries as non-negotiable; they are crucial for trust and safety. Then, delve into soft limits, those areas that might be open to exploration but require caution. Approach these with care, dipping a toe in rather than diving in headfirst. It's equally important to address triggers, whether they're emotional, physical, or anything else that could unexpectedly disrupt the experience. Being aware of these in advance can prevent misunderstandings and keep the energy flowing. Finally, talk about goals—what each person hopes to feel, achieve, or explore during the scene. These open, honest conversations aren't just about logistics; they set the tone for connection, trust, and shared understanding.

Safe words aren't just for beginners—they're the unsung heroes of every scene. Use a simple traffic-light system:

- Red: Stop everything immediately.
- Yellow: Slow down or reduce intensity.
- Green: Full steam ahead.

For non-verbal signals (e.g., if gags are involved), establish alternatives like tapping out or dropping an object. Because nothing kills the mood like, "Mmmph mmmph!" and you realizing you forgot the signal.

Warm-Ups and Mindset Preparation

Imagine beginning a workout by attempting to deadlift your maximum weight without any prior preparation—it would be painful and unwise. The same principle applies to BDSM. Warm-ups are not just helpful; they are absolutely essential. They serve to prepare the body by increasing circulation and sensitivity, ease the submissive into the proper headspace, and build a sense of delicious anticipation. Start the process slowly and seductively. Use gentle spanking or stroking to awaken nerve endings, run feathers or other light tools across their skin to tease and excite, and gradually increase the intensity to establish the desired tone. Equally important is getting into the right mindset, as this makes all the difference. Guide your submissive with clear and commanding instructions such as, "Kneel here and don't move," or tease them with verbal cues like, "Do you have any idea what's coming? No? Perfect." Incorporating deep breathing exercises can also help them relax and focus, ensuring they are fully present and ready to engage.

Punishment Spotlight

Preparation isn't just practical—it's a seduction in itself. Take your time laying out your tools with care, treating each one like a sacred object. As your submissive watches, explain the purpose of each item, letting your words tease and tantalize while building anticipation. Once the stage is set, guide your submissive to kneel or assume their starting position. Blindfold them to strip away distractions, sharpening their focus and amplifying their anticipation. When you're ready, introduce the first tool slowly, letting them feel its weight, texture, or temperature before you begin. Every detail should heighten their senses and their surrender. To avoid breaking the spell, steer clear of common missteps. Never skip negotiation—even experienced partners need to reaffirm boundaries and expectations. Don't rush the warm-up; anticipation is the fuel that makes the scene burn hotter. And simplicity is key—this isn't the time to debut your juggling act or overcomplicate the experience. Preparation is more than a step; it's the foundation of every unforgettable

Preparing for Punishment Setting the Stage for Success

scene. With the right tools, clear communication, and a carefully crafted atmosphere, you're not just delivering punishment—you're creating an artful, intimate masterpiece. Now that the stage is set, let the fun begin.

Chapter 1

The Whisper Challenge – Words They'll Never Forget

Imagine a punishment where every word matters, but they can barely hear you. The Whisper Challenge is all about forcing your submissive to focus, listen, and hang on to every syllable. If they fail to repeat your words exactly, they face the consequences.

This punishment is a mix of psychological dominance, sensory play, and creative humiliation. It's subtle, intimate, and oh-so-effective.

Why Whisper Challenge Works

The Whisper Challenge is a masterclass in subtle domination, and it works on several irresistible levels. First, it forces heightened focus. With every whispered command, your submissive must pay close attention, hanging on your every word. There's no room for distraction, and that laser-sharp concentration pulls them deeper into submission with each passing second.

Then, there's the sensory manipulation. Whispering creates an intensely private, intimate power dynamic, where every word feels like it's meant just for them. Your voice becomes the only thing that matters, wrapping around them like a velvet leash. The act of straining to hear, combined with the closeness of your presence, builds an atmosphere that's electric with control.

Finally, the fun really ramps up with mistake-driven punishment. The more they stumble or get it wrong, the more excuses you have to dish out creative corrections. Whether it's a teasing scolding, a playful swat, or another round of whispering just to keep them on edge, their errors become part of the game—and every mistake only deepens their surrender.

Required Tools & Preparation

- A quiet room.
- Earplugs or light music (optional) to make hearing harder.
- A list of words, phrases, or commands.

Execution

Step 1: Establish the Rules

Instruct your submissive to listen carefully and repeat everything you whisper. Make it clear:

"Every mistake you make will earn you another punishment. Let's see how well you pay attention."

Step 2: Begin the Whisper Game

Start by whispering simple phrases. Gradually increase complexity or add humiliation: *"I live to obey you.", "I deserve this punishment.", "I will follow every rule."* Speak softly enough to make them strain to hear, but not so quietly they're completely lost.

Step 3: Enforce Mistakes
For every word or phrase they miss, assign a consequence:

- Spanks for every missed word.
- Holding a position for each mistake.
- Restarting the entire challenge.

Step 4: Raise the Stakes
Introduce tongue-twisters, foreign languages, or nonsense phrases to make it even harder. The goal isn't perfection—it's control.

Punishment Spotlight

Set the scene by having your submissive kneel in front of you, their focus entirely on your voice. To heighten the challenge, have them wear earplugs, forcing them to strain to hear each word. Whisper sentences into their ear, starting simple and gradually becoming more complex, and demand they repeat each one word-for-word. Every mistake becomes an opportunity for correction, and every success brings them closer to earning your approval. Begin with a soft, straightforward whisper, such as, "I will do better." It's an easy phrase to ease them into the task, but don't let them get too comfortable. Slowly raise the stakes, introducing longer, more intricate sentences like, "I humbly accept my Dominant's discipline without question." Missteps are inevitable, and that's where you come in—pause to administer a punishment that reinforces their focus, whether it's a swat, a pinch, or a moment of playful scolding. Continue until they've nailed the phrase perfectly, ensuring every moment is filled with delicious tension.

Pro-Level Variations

For an added challenge, combine this exercise with a physical task. Have them balance on their knees, hold a plank, or even carry an object as they struggle to repeat your words. The combination of mental focus and physical endurance turns the scene into a full-body experience. If you're feeling particularly daring, take the game into a public setting—whisper commands at a restaurant or during a walk, where they must obey discreetly without drawing attention. To tease and torment, consider offering small rewards for their accuracy—a light caress, a word of praise—only to snatch them away at the first sign of failure.

Safety Tips

Keep the exercise engaging but not overly demanding. Whisper durations should be short enough to maintain focus but not so long that they create frustration or fatigue. If earplugs are part of the scene, ensure they can still hear you at a comfortable volume—this is about submission, not sensory deprivation. Be mindful of the content of the whispered phrases; avoid anything overly humiliating unless it has been explicitly negotiated and agreed upon in advance. As always, watch for signs of discomfort and be ready to adjust as needed to keep the experience enjoyable and safe for both of you.

Aftercare

After the challenge, praise their efforts and acknowledge their focus. If the punishment involved complex commands, offer a moment of lightheartedness to relieve tension.

The Point

The Whisper Challenge is a masterclass in subtle dominance. It's intimate, clever, and guaranteed to make your submissive hang on your every word—literally.

Chapter 2

The Countdown Confession – Tick-Tock and Talk

What happens when a punishment blends mental pressure, physical endurance, and a touch of humiliation? Meet the Countdown Confession, a punishment that forces your submissive to confess their mistakes within a limited time—or face escalating consequences. It's part interrogation, part endurance test, and entirely under your control. This unique punishment flips the script by putting the focus on their accountability while keeping them on edge. Each second of hesitation is a second closer to their doom (or at least, another round of torment).

Why Countdown Confession Works

The Countdown Confession thrives on its psychological intensity and the layers of accountability it demands. The ticking clock applies mental pressure, forcing quick thinking and immediate submission. The act of confessing requires them to actively confront their mistakes, turning the punishment into a meaningful exercise rather than a simple act of discipline. And because the consequences can be customized, you're free to tailor the experience to their limits and your preferences, adding physical challenges to heighten the tension.

Required Tools & Preparation

- A timer (or your commanding voice as the countdown).
- A chair or kneeling position for focus.
- Optional props: paddles, weights, or anything to enforce consequences.

Execution

Step 1: Establish the Rules

Set the scene with a commanding tone: *"You have 60 seconds to confess what you did wrong. Every second you waste is another punishment added. Fail to confess, and I'll decide for you."* Make sure they understand the stakes—this is their chance to own up.

Step 2: Start the Timer

Begin the countdown. Stand nearby, silently watching as they scramble for words. The pressure builds with every passing second.

Step 3: Impose Consequences

For every second they fail to confess, add a punishment: Extra spanks or strikes; Holding a position for an additional minute; Repeating the countdown until they confess fully.

Step 4: Final Judgment

Once the confession is complete, decide if it's good enough—or if they need to pay for their hesitation anyway. (Spoiler: They probably do.)

Punishment Spotlight

Put your submissive in a kneeling position, set the timer for 30 seconds, and let the countdown begin. Their task? Confess their sins before the buzzer goes off. If they fail? Oh, that's where the fun begins. Maybe they hold a heavy object until their arms shake, maybe they feel the sting of a paddle, or maybe they get to enjoy the honor of starting the countdown all over again. The choice is yours, and let's be honest, they'll love every second of it —even if they're too flustered to admit it. Execution is key here. Start with an intimidating stare as the timer ticks down. Don't say a word, just let the silence mess with their head. As the tension builds, lean in with a smirk and tease them a little: "Nothing yet? Should I start taking guesses for you?" As the timer winds down, ramp up the drama by counting aloud, slow and deliberate, like you're savoring their growing panic. Watching them scramble to confess before the buzzer is half the fun—and the other half is deciding what happens when they don't.

Pro-Level Variations

Want to spice it up? Throw in a Surprise Confession—hit them with the countdown out of nowhere, maybe mid-scene or when they least expect it. Nothing gets the adrenaline pumping like realizing the clock is already ticking. Or go for a Physical Countdown: make them hold a plank or squat while they confess. Suddenly, admitting they forgot to clean the toys seems a lot harder when their legs are shaking. Feeling extra devious? Try Timed Questions—for every second they waste, make them answer a humiliating question. "What's the most embarrassing thing you've ever done in public? Quick, go!" Watching them stammer through a mix of confessions and questions adds a whole new layer of fun (for you) and mortification (for them).

Safety Tips

This punishment is intense, so don't go overboard. A countdown should be short enough to build pressure but not so long that it leaves them overwhelmed. If they start looking genuinely distressed, ease up. The goal is to challenge, not to crush their spirit (unless that's their thing). And remember, this isn't an everyday kind of punishment—keep it special, like a surprise dessert. Monitor their reactions and always be ready to switch gears if needed. After all, a happy, slightly frazzled submissive is the best kind.

Aftercare

Reassure them that confessing was brave and important. Remind them that the punishment was about growth, not cruelty. Offer physical comfort to ease any lingering tension.

The Point

The Countdown Confession is a unique blend of mental and physical challenge that reinforces their accountability—and keeps you firmly in control.

Chapter 3

Ordeal Tasks – Where Discipline Meets Evil Genius

Let's be real—sometimes the best punishments are the ones that make your submissive *think* about what's coming while dreading every second of it. Enter ordeal tasks, the ultimate combination of mental torture and creative genius. Whether it's holding a ridiculous pose, scrubbing floors like a character from a melodramatic soap opera, or writing "I'm sorry" a hundred times like they're back in detention, ordeal tasks keep things interesting. The beauty? You're in complete control, they're squirming, and the possibilities are endless. Plus, you get to feel like a diabolical mastermind, which is a nice perk.

Why Ordeals Work

Ordeals are the perfect blend of challenge, trust, and just a little bit of sadistic fun. They work because they mess with your submissive's mind in the best possible way. It's all about mental mayhem—dangling the proverbial carrot, except the carrot is a punishment, and they know it's going to be rough. The anticipation, the build-up, the sheer *oh no, what have I agreed to* moment—it's all part of the thrill. Watching them wrestle with their own determination as they inch closer to the inevitable is half the fun. There's also something deeply satisfying about testing their physical prowess. Let's face it, sometimes you just want to see them sweat. Whether it's holding an impossible position or navigating a Lego-strewn gauntlet, their effort becomes a performance of submission and endurance that's hard to resist. The physicality of an ordeal pushes them to their limits while letting you revel in the power exchange. But at the heart of it all, ordeals are a bonding experience. It takes an incredible amount of trust for a submissive to willingly take on something difficult—whether it's enduring discomfort, overcoming fear, or simply walking barefoot on Legos because you said so. That willingness to endure for you, and your care in guiding them through it, strengthens the connection between Dominant and submissive in a way that's as profound as it is playful.

Required Tools & Preparation

Here's your shopping list for turning your submissive into a task-finishing machine:

- Paper and pen (if writing punishments are your jam).
- A timer to make sure they feel every agonizing second.
- Props for tasks: think ice cubes, heavy books, or random household items that suddenly seem sinister.

Execution

Step 1: Design the Ordeal

Think of a task that's challenging, slightly ridiculous, and just punishing enough to remind them who's boss. Some ideas:

- Write their sins 100 times: "I will not forget to address you as Master/Mistress" on repeat. (Bonus: It'll haunt their dreams.)
- Ridiculous chores: Scrub the floor on all fours with a toothbrush.
- Endurance stunts: Hold a plank position while reciting Shakespeare.

Step 2: Lay Down the Law

When you give instructions, channel your inner drill sergeant. This is not the time for "pretty please." Be precise, be firm, and, above all, be creative. Example Script: *"You will kneel in the corner and balance this book on your head for 15 minutes. If it falls, we start over. Don't disappoint me. Or do—I'd love to watch you try again."*

Step 3: Enjoy the Show

Sit back, relax, and bask in your brilliance. Whether it's holding a pose or writing an essay on why they shouldn't sass you, watching their dedication is part of the fun.

If they falter, remind them who's in charge. A simple *"Did I say you could move?"* goes a long way.

Step 4: Judge, Jury, Executioner

When the task is done, decide if they succeeded. If yes, give them a nod of approval or a pat on the head (if you're feeling generous). If they fail, restart or level up the punishment.

Punishment Spotlight

your submissive, arms outstretched, holding an ice cube in each hand like a frosty T-pose of remorse. The goal? Endure five minutes of chilly, trembling endurance without dropping them—or shedding a single tear. It's a test of willpower, physical strength, and maybe a little bit of theatrical suffering, all while you sit back and enjoy the show. To begin, hand them the ice cubes and point to their designated spot. With a calm but firm tone, set the stage: "If the ice falls, we start over. And no, dripping water doesn't count as tears." Then, set the timer and let the punishment unfold. Watch as their shivering determination grows more desperate by the second, their arms trembling as they fight the urge to give in. Meanwhile, you sip your tea (or wine) with an air of amused detachment, savoring every moment of their effort. If they drop the ice before the timer dings? Reset the clock with a slow, wicked grin and watch the frustration build.

Safety First

Don't let their hands freeze off. You want to punish them, not send them to the ER.

Pro-Level Variations

For those moments when you're feeling particularly devious, try leveling up the challenge. Introduce The Balancing Act, where they must hold a tray of water glasses along with the ice cubes, ensuring not a single drop spills. The combined tension of balance and cold will leave them quaking in more ways than one. Or, if you're feeling creative, throw in The Lego Gauntlet. Blindfold them and make them navigate a path of LEGO bricks while still clutching their icy burdens. Every misstep will have them questioning all their life choices. For a final twist, go with Writing With a Twist, where they must complete a task like writing lines or drawing—using their non-dominant hand. It's slow, awkward, and just embarrassing enough to make it memorable.

Aftercare

Punishment's over, and now it's time to be nice again (ugh, fine). Wrap them up in a blanket, tell them they did well (or at least tried), and remind them why they trust you.

The Point

Ordeal tasks are more than just punishment they're an art form. Done right, they leave your submissive humbled, amused, and weirdly satisfied. Plus, they'll think twice before breaking your rules again. Now go forth, dear Dominant, and wield your newfound genius like the benevolent tyrant you are.

Chapter 4

Impact Play – When Words Aren't Enough

Sometimes, actions speak louder than words—especially when those actions involve a flogger, paddle, or your own perfectly calibrated hand. Welcome to the realm of impact play, where each strike is a conversation, each mark a signature, and each yelp of surprise a standing ovation to your expertise.

Impact play is a staple of BDSM punishments, blending physical sensation, emotional intensity, and a dash of drama. Done right, it's not just about pain—it's about connection, trust, and leaving your submissive exactly where you want them: exhilarated, humbled, and maybe just a little tender.

Why Impact Play Works

Impact play is a classic for a reason—it's immediate, versatile, and visually striking. One of the biggest reasons it's so effective is the instant feedback it provides. Every smack, swat, or thud delivers results right away: satisfaction for you as the Dominant and a delicious mix of sensations for them. There's no waiting, no wondering if your point landed—because it most certainly did. The sound alone is enough to make the moment electric, but the physical reaction seals the deal.

Another reason impact play is so captivating is its customizable intensity. You're completely in control of how far you take it. From light, teasing taps that leave them giggling to harder strikes that elicit a gasp or a moan, you can tailor the experience to suit the mood, the scene, and your partner's preferences. And if you're the type who enjoys a lasting impression, you can always push for that "oh wow, that's going to bruise" sweet spot—because nothing says satisfaction like a mark that lingers. Finally, let's talk about the aesthetic appeal. There's something undeniably beautiful about a well-placed handprint, the flush of reddened skin, or the delicate marks left by a paddle or flogger. It's art in motion, a visual reminder of your dominance and their submission. Impact play engages all the senses—sight, sound, and touch—making it a dynamic and powerful tool in any BDSM scene.

Required Tools & Preparation

Your toolbox will depend on the vibe you're going for. Start with:

- Bare Hands: The classic. Always available, zero cost, highly effective.
- Paddles: Wood, leather, or silicone, each with its own unique feel and sound.
- Floggers: For those who want to add a touch of theatrical flair.
- Canes: Advanced users only. Precision is key.
- Straps/Belts: Multipurpose and delivers that satisfying *snap*.

Execution

Step 1: The Setup

Pick a position that ensures comfort and stability. Options include: Bent over a sturdy surface; Kneeling with hands on the floor; Lying flat with pillows for support. Explain the rules clearly. Example: *"You'll stay in this position until I'm done. If you move, we start over. Got it?"*

Step 2: Test the Waters

Always start light. Warm up the area with a few soft strikes to build anticipation and get the blood flowing. Think of it as preheating the oven—you don't just crank it to 500°F and hope for the best.

Step 3: Deliver the Punishment

Vary your strikes—mix up the rhythm, force, and location to keep them guessing. A few tips:

- Backside: A classic. Plenty of cushion and nerves for maximum effect.
- Thighs: A bit more sting and a lot more vulnerability.
- Soles of the Feet: For the adventurous (and masochistic).

Pro Tip: Pause occasionally. Let the anticipation build. Few things are more powerful than hearing them whisper, *"Is that it?"* only to respond with, *"Not even close."*

Step 4: Wrap It Up

Decide when they've had enough (and no, "one more for good luck" doesn't count as restraint). End with a softer touch—a caress, a soothing word, or a gentle rub over the punished area.

Punishment Spotlight

Grab your favorite paddle—or a spatula, if you're in the mood for something a little more domestic—and position your submissive over a sturdy surface. The scene is set, the tension is palpable, and it's time to make your point with precision, care, and just the right amount of sting. Start with a few light strikes to warm them up. Think of it as stretching before a workout—this isn't the time to go full force. Gradually build intensity, aiming for that delicious moment where they gasp in surprise but lean into the sensation, not away from it. Between strikes, keep the suspense alive. Tease them with light touches, your fingers tracing the warm skin you've just marked, or let your voice do the work. A well-timed line like, *"This is what happens when you forget my instructions. Will you remember now?"* can go a long way toward keeping their mind as engaged as their body. Finish the session with care. Leave them marked but not broken, their skin a canvas of your dominance. Step back and admire your work—it's art, after all, and every stroke is a testament to your control.

Pro-Level Variations

For an extra layer of tension, try The Countdown. Tell them they're in for 10 strikes, but just when they think it's over, add an unexpected bonus strike. The surprise will keep them on edge and remind them who's in charge. If you're feeling experimental, go for Double Trouble. Alternate between two tools, like a paddle and a flogger, to create a mix of sensations that keeps them guessing.

For a sensory twist, combine impact with contrast. After each strike, introduce an ice cube or soft fabric to the area you've just marked. The sudden switch from sharp sting to soothing coolness heightens their sensitivity and turns every moment into an unforgettable experience.

Safety Tips

Impact play is thrilling, but safety is always the priority. Avoid bony areas like the spine or joints, sticking to the fleshy parts that can handle the impact. Watch their reactions closely—both verbal and non-verbal—to gauge their comfort level. Before you start, agree on safe words and make sure they know how to use them. If you hear "red," everything stops immediately. Remember, the best punishments challenge but never cross the line into harm.

Aftercare

Post-impact play is where the magic happens. Offer cuddles, lotion for any marks, and a chance to talk about the experience. Compliment their endurance—it's good for morale.

The Point

Impact play isn't about inflicting pain; it's about creating an experience. Whether you're using your hand, a paddle, or a bit of both, remember: every strike is a conversation, and you're both here to enjoy the dialogue.

Chapter 5

Sensory Deprivation – Silence is Golden

Ever wanted to make your submissive's world go completely dark? Sensory deprivation is like putting them in time-out, but way more intense—and much more fun. By limiting their senses, you take total control of their perception. Blindfolds, earplugs, and even hoods can be your tools of choice, turning their world into a playground of uncertainty (and your playground of domination). This technique pairs beautifully with other punishments or as a standalone method to make them squirm. It's simple, elegant, and dripping with power.

Why Sensory Deprivation Works

Sensory deprivation is a masterstroke in control, stripping away distractions and plunging your submissive into a world where only you exist. The first reason it works so well is the total focus it demands. With their vision obscured, their hearing muffled, or both, your submissive has no choice but to cling to every word, sound, or touch you offer. It's like flipping a switch in their brain

—everything else fades away, and you become the sole center of their attention.

Then comes the magic of heightened reactions. Take away sight or sound, and suddenly even the lightest brush of your fingertips feels electric. Every sensation is amplified, every touch leaves a deeper imprint. A single whispered word or a gentle stroke can send shivers through their entire body, creating an atmosphere that's intensely intimate and charged with anticipation.

But the real beauty of sensory deprivation lies in how it deepens their submission. By taking away their control over their own senses, you reinforce your dominance in the most tangible way. They're no longer in charge of how or when they experience the world around them—that's entirely up to you. It's a profound act of trust that strengthens the bond between you and makes every moment of the scene unforgettable.

Required Tools & Preparation

- Blindfolds: Keep it soft but snug. No peeking allowed!
- Earplugs or Headphones: Silence is key—or blast something unexpected.
- Hoods: Advanced option for full sensory blackout.
- Optional: Feather, ice cubes, flogger, or anything to add extra surprises.

Execution

Step 1: Prep the Submissive

Explain what's going to happen. Build their anticipation with a tone of authority: *"For the next 30 minutes, you won't see, hear, or control anything. Your only job is to obey and feel."* Get consent beforehand—this isn't the time for surprises.

Step 2: Apply Deprivation Tools

Secure the blindfold to block their vision. Add earplugs or noise-canceling headphones to cut out sound. Test their limits by asking, *"Can you see? Can you hear me?"* Adjust as needed.

Step 3: Play With Their Vulnerability

Once deprived of their senses, use their heightened awareness to your advantage:

- Whisper commands or tease them with silence.
- Introduce sensations like a cold ice cube trailing across their skin or the sharp snap of a flogger.
- Take pauses to leave them hanging in suspense—it's cruel but oh-so-effective.

Step 4: Finish With Flair

Gradually bring them back. Remove earplugs first, then the blindfold, and let them process the experience. A simple, *"Good job,"* goes a long way.

Punishment Spotlight

The Stillness Challenge is a test of discipline, endurance, and submission all rolled into one. The setup is deceptively simple: blindfold your submissive, block their hearing, and command them to remain perfectly still. No fidgeting, no shifting, no sneaky little movements. The catch? If they move, the punishment starts over from the beginning. It's a game of patience—for them—and control—for you. Begin by setting the scene with sensory deprivation tools. A blindfold and noise-canceling headphones or earplugs will do the trick, plunging your submissive into a world where they can focus only on their body and your presence. Once they're prepped, use a mix of sensations to test their resolve. A soft feather trailing down their arm, a teasing brush against their skin, or the sharp sting of a quick flick with a cane—all are fair game. The goal is to push them to the brink without allowing them to break the stillness. And if they move? Reset the timer with an air of amused authority. They'll quickly realize that you're fully in charge, and their only option is to surrender completely to your rules.

Pro-Level Variations

For a more advanced twist, introduce temperature play into the mix. Alternate between ice cubes and the warmth of your hands, contrasting sensations to challenge their control. To increase their helplessness, add light bondage, such as wrist or ankle restraints, ensuring they're truly at your mercy. Feeling extra playful? Try tickling torment—a gentle tease of their most sensitive spots is guaranteed to make staying still an almost impossible task.

Safety Tips

While this challenge can be a thrilling test of endurance, it's important to prioritize safety. Always ensure your submissive can breathe comfortably, and avoid leaving them in full sensory deprivation for too long—10 to 15 minutes is a good starting point. Check in frequently using non-verbal cues, such as a squeeze of the hand, to confirm they're comfortable and still enjoying the experience. Your goal is to challenge them, not to overwhelm them, so stay attuned to their reactions throughout.

Aftercare

Bring them back to reality with care. A warm drink, soft touch, and soothing words will help them feel safe and grounded.

The Point

Sensory deprivation takes away their world, leaving them completely at your mercy. It's intimate, powerful, and unforgettable. If you're ready to own every inch of their experience, this one's for you.

Chapter 6

Chastity as Punishment – Lock It Down

Sometimes, the best punishment isn't what you do to your submissive but what you *don't let them do*. Enter chastity: the ultimate in delayed gratification and control. By locking away their pleasure, you turn submission into a test of patience, obedience, and sheer willpower.

Whether it's a chastity cage, belt, or a simple "hands-off" command, chastity punishes by taking away the one thing they want most—and giving you all the power.

Why Chastity Works

Chastity is the ultimate game of patience, power, and control, and it works because it flips the script on instant gratification. First and foremost, it builds anticipation like nothing else. Denial has a way of making the heart—and let's be real, other parts—grow fonder. Every day locked away is another day of simmering tension, where they're counting the seconds until you decide they've earned their release. It's like dangling the world's most enticing carrot just out of reach, and trust me, they're thinking about it. Constantly.

Then there's the way chastity reinforces control. Once they're locked up, every second becomes about you. You're no longer just their Dominant; you're the gatekeeper of their pleasure, the all-powerful deity deciding when (or if) they'll be allowed a taste of freedom. That little cage isn't just physical—it's a mental reminder that they're yours, completely and utterly, with every ache and longing thought tethered to your decisions.

And the best part? Chastity keeps things creative. It's not just about locking them up and walking away; it's about the games, the teases, the tasks that keep them squirming on the edge. Have them write daily devotionals, complete challenges to earn points, or simply send them a suggestive text at the most inconvenient moment. The possibilities are endless, and so is their frustration. Let's face it, chastity isn't just a punishment—it's an art form, and you're the master

Required Tools & Preparation

- Chastity Devices: Choose one that fits comfortably but securely.
- Locks and Keys: Symbolic and practical—you hold all the power.

Execution

Step 1: Introduction

Start with a teasing explanation: *"You've shown you can't control yourself, so I'll do it for you. This is your reminder of who's in charge."*

Step 2: Apply the Device

Ensure the device fits properly and isn't causing discomfort.

Lock it securely and make a show of keeping the key—it's all about the power dynamic.

Step 3: Set the Rules

Lay down your conditions:

- Duration: An hour? A day? A week?
- Behavior: Will they have to earn their release?
- Tasks: Assign tasks that make them "prove" their submission.

Step 4: Tease and Torment

Throughout their chastity, remind them of their predicament. A casual whisper, *"How's that cage feeling?"* can drive them wild.

Punishment Spotlight

Start by locking your submissive in a chastity device for 24 hours. The key is to keep their mind as engaged as their body, so assign tasks throughout the day that reinforce their submission and remind them who's in charge. It's not just about the physical restriction—it's about the constant, simmering tension that builds with every passing hour. Begin the day with a simple yet authoritative act: lock them up and make your expectations crystal clear. A few carefully chosen words—like "I'll decide when you've earned your freedom"—set the tone for the hours ahead. As the day unfolds, keep them on edge with periodic check-ins. Send a playful tease, assign a quick task, or drop an unexpected command that reminds them of their place. The anticipation of what's next becomes part of the punishment, keeping their mind spinning with thoughts of you. When the day ends, you hold all the power. If they've earned it, you might grant a release—but only after savoring their relief and gratitude. Or, if you're feeling particularly wicked, extend their chastity sentence. After all, the sweetest torment is the one they didn't see coming.

Pro-Level Variations

For an extra layer of excitement, introduce public chastity. It's subtle enough for daily life, but the secret thrill of knowing they're locked up while running errands or attending meetings adds a delicious edge. To make things more playful, try a game of *Key Hunt*. Hide the key and create a series of tasks or riddles they must complete to earn its location—because nothing says submission like working for your freedom. And for the ultimate challenge, pair chastity with an ordeal task. Imagine them holding a plank or navigating a tricky obstacle while still locked up. It's double the punishment and double the fun.

Safety Tips

While chastity can be thrilling, it's essential to prioritize safety. Make sure the device is comfortable, fits correctly, and doesn't restrict circulation. If your submissive is new to chastity, avoid extended wear—start small and gradually build up to longer durations. Throughout the day, check in frequently to ensure both their physical and mental well-being. The goal is to push their limits, not to cause harm. With care and attention, chastity becomes not just a punishment, but a powerful tool for trust, control, and connection.

Aftercare

Celebrate their endurance with positive reinforcement. Whether it's physical, verbal, or a well-deserved release, let them feel appreciated for their submission.

The Point

Chastity is the ultimate reminder of your power. Whether it's for an hour or a week, this punishment keeps them focused on you—and nothing else.

Chapter 7

Writing Assignments – Words of Regret

Sometimes, the best punishment isn't physical—it's making them confront their behavior with pen and paper. Writing assignments are a brilliant way to combine discipline, reflection, and a little creative humiliation. Plus, it's the perfect excuse to have them write something as absurd as a 500-word essay on "Why I Should Obey."

Why Writing Assignments Work

Writing assignments are a powerful tool in discipline because they engage the submissive on multiple levels. They pose a mental challenge by requiring the submissive to actively reflect on their actions and the reasons behind them. This form of punishment also introduces an element of embarrassment, as the sillier the assigned topic, the more uncomfortable and self-conscious they are likely to feel. Perhaps most importantly, the process makes the lesson unforgettable. The effort and discomfort involved ensure they will think carefully before repeating the behavior that led to the assignment in the first place.

Required Tools & Preparation

- Notebook or paper.
- Pen (preferably one that works—you're punishing them, not yourself).

Execution

Step 1: Assign the Task
Choose a topic that fits the crime: "10 Reasons I Should Follow the Rules"; "Why My Dom is Always Right"; A letter of apology with extra flair.

Step 2: Set the Rules
Be specific about length, style, and tone. Example: *"500 words. Legible. No whining. Due in an hour."*

Step 3: Collect and Review
Read it aloud—or make them read it to you. Correct their grammar for extra humiliation.

Step 4: Decide the Next Step
If it's not up to standard, assign another. Or escalate to a physical punishment for added motivation.

Punishment Spotlight

Make them craft a deeply heartfelt, painfully detailed apology for their misbehavior—no shortcuts, no excuses, and absolutely no fewer than 300 words. Here's how to make it stick. Start by laying down the rules: give them the topic, set a firm deadline, and make it clear that anything less than genuine effort will only make things worse. When they turn it in, don't just read it—scrutinize every word like a disappointed teacher grading a failing essay. And for that extra flair? Whip out a red pen and ruthlessly mark every mistake, crossing out lazy phrasing, and circling typos with exaggerated disapproval. Watch as the weight of their words sinks in, one red slash at a time.

Pro-Level Variations

For a bold move, try public sharing. With their consent, post the essay somewhere it can be seen by others, ensuring an extra layer of embarrassment that sticks with them long after the ink dries. If that feels too tame, demand illustrated essays. Have them pair their words with hand-drawn diagrams, charts, or doodles that match the theme of their writing. Whether it's a cringe-worthy flowchart of "Why I Should Listen" or a stick-figure storyboard of their misbehavior, the added effort makes the punishment even more unforgettable—and delightfully absurd.

Safety Tips

Be mindful of topics that could trigger negative emotions. Keep it light-hearted if appropriate—humour goes a long way.

Aftercare

Praise their effort (or lack thereof) and offer reassurance. They've earned it, even if their essay was riddled with typos.

The Point

Writing assignments are proof that punishment doesn't always require a paddle. Sometimes, a pen and a little creativity are all you need to remind them who's boss.

Chapter 8

Public Embarrassment – Subtle Thrills in the Real World

Want to keep your submissive on their toes without anyone catching on? Public embarrassment is your go-to punishment. It's the ultimate stealth move—discreet, thrilling, and guaranteed to make your submissive blush in all the right ways. Whether it's a whispered command, a hidden toy, or a secret rule, you can remind them who's in charge while the rest of the world is blissfully unaware.

Why Public Embarrassment Works

Public embarrassment works because it taps into powerful emotions and deepens the dynamic in unexpected ways. The heightened awareness that comes from the risk of being noticed turns every moment into a charged experience, amplifying intensity and keeping them on edge. There's also the emotional thrill—those subtle, covert acts of dominance remind them of their place and keep the dynamic alive far beyond the bedroom. Best of all, it fosters a private connection between the two of you. Only you know the full story, creating an intimate secret that binds you closer while leaving them deliciously flustered.

Required Tools & Preparation

- Simple props (e.g., a small vibrator, discreet restraints).
- A public setting where you both feel safe and comfortable.
- Confidence and creativity—you're running the show, after all.

Execution

Step 1: Set the Rules

Before you step out, establish the boundaries. Example:
"You will address me as 'Sir' at all times today—quietly, of course. And if you forget? That's one strike against you."

Step 2: Choose the Punishment

Pick something subtle but effective:

- Having them wear an outfit or accessory of your choosing.
- Assigning secret rules like no sitting without permission.
- Using a remote-controlled toy (hello, technology!) during your outing.

Step 3: Enforce the Rules

Throughout the day, remind them of your control with quiet commands or teasing looks. If they break a rule, lean in and whisper: *"That's two strikes. Care to go for three?"*

Step 4: End With a Bang

When the punishment is complete, acknowledge their obedience—or add another layer of embarrassment by reviewing their infractions aloud once you're alone.

Punishment Spotlight

Turn up the heat during a dinner date by setting a simple rule: your submissive can't speak unless directly addressed. If they slip up, they owe you a penalty—like holding your bag on the way home, because nothing says "lesson learned" like being your personal valet. Quietly remind them of the rule as the evening begins, setting the stage for delicious tension. Then, keep them on their toes by teasing them with unexpected questions or catching them off-guard with sly comments. Tally up their infractions for a full post-date review—because nothing adds suspense like wondering just how much trouble they're in.

Pro-Level Variations

For extra spice, incorporate a hidden toy thrill by sneaking in a remote-controlled vibrator during mundane errands—because groceries are more fun with a side of secret chaos. Or mark them in public with a subtle token of your choosing, like a discreet bracelet or collar that screams "theirs" without shouting it to the world. If you want a creative touch, assign a covert writing task: make them scrawl "I will obey" in hidden spots throughout the day—on napkins, receipts, or any surface that makes them squirm with nervous delight.

Safety Tips

Always ensure the setting is safe and low-risk. Public punishment should keep the tension between you two without involving unwilling participants. Subtlety is your best friend—because less is always more when it comes to keeping things classy and thrilling. And above all, stay tuned to their comfort level, ready to adjust if things get overwhelming. After all, the goal is mutual enjoyment, not public disaster.

Aftercare

Once you're back in private, reward their efforts and let them unwind. Public punishment can be intense, so offer reassurance and comfort to rebuild their confidence.

The Point

Public embarrassment is about subtle control and shared intimacy. It's not about making a scene—it's about reminding them, with every glance and word, that they belong to you.

Chapter 9

The Gag Challenge – Silence Is Punishment

Sometimes, the best way to punish your submissive is to take away their voice. Enter the gag challenge, a simple but highly effective punishment that forces them to communicate without words. Whether it's a ball gag, bit gag, or even a makeshift scarf, this punishment leaves them powerless and entirely at your mercy.

Why Gag Challenges Work

Gag challenges bring a whole new level of control and intensity to the scene. First, there's the enforced silence—nothing screams "I'm in charge" like stripping them of their ability to speak. It's a power move that sets the tone instantly. Then, there's the heightened sensation. With their mouth occupied, their focus shifts entirely to the other senses, making every touch, whisper, or glance feel electrifying. Finally, let's not forget the visual appeal. A gag just looks undeniably good on them, and deep down, they know it too—adding an extra layer of vulnerability and allure that's impossible to resist.

Required Tools & Preparation

- Gags (ball, bit, or tape for variety).
- Timer to set the duration.
- Optional: Tasks they must complete while gagged (writing, signals, etc.).

Execution

Step 1: Select the Gag

Choose a gag based on the level of restriction you want. For example: Ball gags for silence with a bit of drool (bonus embarrassment); Bit gags for a slightly softer look; Tape for full domination vibes.

Step 2: Give the Rules

Explain their challenge. Example: *"You'll wear this gag for 15 minutes. During that time, you'll follow my every instruction. Any failure will add 5 more minutes."*

Step 3: Introduce Tasks

Make the punishment interactive:

- They must follow hand signals or written commands.
- Add a physical challenge like holding a position.
- Use sensory play (touch, tease, or tickle) to test their reactions.

Step 4: Monitor and Adjust

Keep an eye on their comfort level. If they're doing well, tease them by extending the time or adding tasks. If they're struggling, guide them back gently.

Punishment Spotlight

Put their obedience—and their penmanship—to the test by having them write a message while gagged. The catch? If it's messy or incomplete, the timer resets, and they start over. How to Pull It Off. Begin by gagging them and placing a pen and paper in front of them, ensuring everything is within reach. Assign a simple but pointed phrase like, "I'm sorry for disobeying." Once they've finished, review their work with dramatic flair, critiquing every wobble and smudge like a condescending art critic.

Pro-Level Variations

Up the stakes with timed silence. Add a ticking clock to create pressure and heighten their anticipation. For an extra layer of difficulty, blindfold them while gagged, turning the challenge into a full sensory puzzle. Or introduce an obedience drill, testing their ability to interpret and follow non-verbal commands while they're focused on the task.

Safety Tips

Keep a close eye on their breathing—safety always comes first, no exceptions. Limit the duration of the gag, especially if they're new to this type of punishment. And above all, prioritize their well-being. Be ready to remove the gag immediately if they show any signs of discomfort, because the only pain involved should be the deliciously consensual kind.

Aftercare

After removing the gag, give them water and soothing words. Being gagged can feel overwhelming, so help them feel secure and cared for.

The Point

The gag challenge is a versatile punishment that mixes control, creativity, and a touch of mischief. Silence may be golden, but their obedience is priceless.

Chapter 10

Tickling Torment – Laugh Till You Obey

Tickling as punishment may sound playful, but trust me, it's the stuff of submissive nightmares—and Dominant dreams. There's nothing quite like watching your submissive squirm, gasp, and dissolve into helpless giggles while you maintain the upper hand. This isn't just fun; it's an art form that teeters on the edge of pleasure, frustration, and complete surrender. The best part? Tickling torment is versatile, requires minimal tools, and can be as innocent or devilish as you like.

Why Tickling Torment Works

Tickling torment is the perfect mix of playful and punishing, making it a go-to tool for creative discipline. The overwhelming sensation of tickling floods their senses, leaving them completely at your mercy with no room for defiance or composure.

It's also a genius combination of playful and ruthless. There's no way they can take themselves seriously when they're laughing uncontrollably, squirming under your touch. The best part? You're in total control of the intensity. Whether it's a light, teasing graze or full-on, laugh-until-you-cry torture, the power is entirely in your hands—and they know it.

Required Tools & Preparation

- Your Hands: The classics never fail.
- Feathers: Soft and sneaky, perfect for teasing.
- Brushes: From paintbrushes to electric ones for added zing.

Execution

Step 1: Positioning Is Key

Make sure your submissive is comfortable but unable to avoid your ticklish wrath. Some ideas: Tied wrists and ankles for maximum vulnerability; Arms raised above their head; Feet exposed, ready for relentless attention.

Step 2: Build Anticipation

Start slow and teasingly. Gently run your fingers or a feather along their ribs, toes, or neck. Let them stew in the suspense, unsure of when you'll strike harder. A simple, *"Oh, did that tickle? Let's see what happens if I try here..."* works wonders.

Step 3: Ramp It Up

Take the intensity to the next level by quickening your movements or introducing tools like brushes or firmer strokes. Focus on classic ticklish zones for maximum effect. The ribs and sides are timeless targets, guaranteed to draw a reaction. The soles of the feet, with their extra sensitivity, often prove to be nearly unbearable. For a more advanced dynamic, the inner thighs provide a mix of sensations that can drive them wild.

Keep the suspense alive by constantly switching tools,

adjusting the pace, and surprising them with new locations. The unpredictability is a crucial part of the torment, making them never quite sure what's coming next.

Step 4: Add Challenges

Want to up the ante? Give them a challenge to complete while being tickled:

- *"Stay perfectly still, or we start over."*
- *"Count to ten without laughing."*
- *"Answer my questions, but no giggling!"*

When they inevitably fail, you have a perfect excuse to keep going.

Punishment Spotlight

Blindfold them. Restrain their feet. And let the ticklish torment begin. Use a feather or your fingers to tease their soles mercilessly—it's diabolical simplicity at its best.

How to Execute Like a Mischievous Genius: Start with an innocent announcement: "This will only last 30 seconds." Then, as they brace themselves, begin slow and gentle, gradually ramping up the intensity. Just as they think it's over, let the timer "mysteriously" reset again... and again. Watch them squirm, laugh, and slowly realize there's absolutely no escape.

Pro-Level Variations

Take it up a notch with an ice and heat combo. Switch between ice cubes and warm brushes to keep their nerves on edge with contrasting sensations. Feeling extra devious? Bring in a partner for a tag-team tickling session—two hands (or more) mean double the chaos. For an even wilder ride, mix in some teasing spanking or other sensory play, creating a rollercoaster of sensations they'll never forget.

Safety Tips

Tickling can quickly shift from fun to overwhelming, so keep a close eye on their reactions. Laughter is fantastic, but make sure they're breathing comfortably—gasping for air isn't part of the plan. Most importantly, maintain clear communication. Safe words or gestures are a must to ensure everything stays consensual, enjoyable, and just the right amount of evil.

Aftercare

After the session, offer water, cuddles, and a chance to breathe. Let them know they handled it well, even if they were a giggling mess. Tickling may seem lighthearted, but it can be physically and emotionally exhausting.

The Point

Tickling torment is a brilliant blend of humor, vulnerability, and control. Whether it's light teasing or all-out laughter-induced chaos, it's a reminder that punishment doesn't always have to be serious to be seriously effective.

Now, go forth and tickle—because laughter, in the right hands, is the ultimate weapon.

Chapter 11

Overstimulation – When Enough Isn't Enough

What's worse than being denied pleasure? Having so much of it that it stops feeling good. Welcome to overstimulation: the punishment where more is *definitely* not better. By pushing your submissive past their limits, you take complete control of their pleasure—or frustration—and watch them squirm as they beg for mercy. Overstimulation is about teetering on the edge between pleasure and punishment, where the line blurs and only you decide when the torment ends.

Why Overstimulation Works

Overstimulation is the ultimate display of control, a tantalizing game where you hold all the power. You get to decide exactly how much is too much, pushing their limits while keeping them teetering on the edge. It's a masterclass in dominance, where the same gentle touch that once made them shiver with pleasure transforms into something almost unbearable after prolonged exposure. The beauty of overstimulation lies in its duality. It's not just about the physical sensations—it's a mental challenge.

Watching their bliss slowly shift to desperation as they squirm and gasp under your command is intoxicating. It's a delicious balance of indulgence and torment, where every moment heightens the connection between y

Required Tools & Preparation

- Vibrators, wands, or other toys with continuous settings.
- Restraints to keep them from escaping.
- Optional: Earplugs or blindfolds to heighten their focus on the sensation.

Execution

Step 1: Set the Stage

Start by securing your submissive in a comfortable but immovable position. Whether they're tied to a bed or restrained in a chair, the key is to keep them where you want them. Explain the rules: *"You'll stay here until I decide you've had enough. Spoiler: It's going to be a while."*

Step 2: Build Them Up

Begin with slow, steady stimulation. Use a vibrator or similar tool and watch as they go from relaxed to squirming. Keep a close eye on their reactions—this is all about pushing boundaries, not breaking them.

Step 3: Overload Their Senses

Once they're nearing their peak, *don't stop*. Instead, increase the intensity:

- Hold the vibrator in place after they've reached their limit.

- Add additional stimulation (e.g., teasing their thighs, neck, or ears).
- Combine sensations with spanking, scratching, or light tickling.

The goal is to push them into that delicious state where they're begging for a break but can't quite form the words.

Step 4: Decide When It's Over

This is your call. Stop when they've reached their breaking point—or push them just a little further to make it unforgettable.

Punishment Spotlight

Secure your submissive firmly in place, their body completely at your mercy, and let the wand vibrator become your tool of exquisite control. Begin with the lowest setting, allowing the subtle vibrations to tease and tantalize, building anticipation with each passing moment. Their breath will hitch, their body will tense, and every nerve will beg for more. Slowly, deliberately, increase the intensity, savoring the way their gasps turn to moans, their body arching as they edge closer to release. When they finally shatter in climax, don't let up. Keep the wand pressed against their trembling body, forcing them to ride the waves of overstimulation as their sensitivity soars to unbearable heights. Watch their every reaction—the quivers, the gasps, the helpless surrender—knowing you hold them completely in your grasp. This is more than just punishment; it's a symphony of control, desire, and submission played out in perfect harmony.

Pro-Level Variations

Take things to the next level by layering sensations and keeping your submissive teetering on the edge of blissful torment. For double stimulation, bring in a second toy to target a different area, amplifying their sensitivity until every inch of their body feels like it's on fire. The mix of sensations will leave them gasping, writhing, and utterly overwhelmed. If you want to sit back and enjoy the spectacle, secure the toy in place and let it do the work for you. Watch as they squirm and gasp under its relentless control, knowing they can't escape the waves of pleasure washing over them. It's a hands-free show designed for maximum effect and your ultimate enjoyment. For the ultimate mind game, combine overstimulation with denial. Push them to the brink with relentless vibrations, only to pull away at the last second, leaving them breathless and desperate. Alternate between giving and taking, keeping them in a constant state of anticipation and surrender, unsure of when they'll finally be allowed release. It's a wickedly satisfying way to assert your dominance and keep them completely at your mercy.

Safety Tips

Always prioritize care and connection during play to ensure the experience remains as enjoyable as it is intense. Keep sessions brief to prevent physical discomfort or emotional exhaustion, remembering that less can often be more when it comes to pushing limits. Stay in constant communication, whether through spoken words, safe words, or pre-agreed non-verbal signals, so you're always tuned into their comfort and consent. Pay close attention to their reactions—every sigh, every movement, every shift in body language—to ensure they're fully immersed and enjoying the experience. Safety and trust are the foundations of every unforgettable moment.

Aftercare

Overstimulation can be intense, so follow up with lots of cuddles, water, and verbal reassurance. Let them know they did well and take time to bring them back to a calm state.

The Point

Overstimulation is about taking control of their pleasure and pushing their boundaries in a safe, consensual way. It's intense, unforgettable, and oh-so-satisfying—for you, of course.

Chapter 12

Denial and Edging – So Close, Yet So Far

If overstimulation is about giving too much, denial and edging are about giving *just enough*—and then yanking it away. Nothing says "I'm in control" like bringing your submissive to the edge of release, only to say, *"Not yet."* It's frustrating, maddening, and oh-so-deliciously cruel.

Why Denial and Edging Work

Denial and edging are the ultimate power plays, turning their desire into a slow-burn obsession that keeps their focus locked entirely on you. By holding them just on the edge of release, you create a delicious tension that heightens their craving with every passing moment. The longer they're denied, the more their need intensifies, making the eventual climax feel explosive—or making their frustration a reward all on its own. At its core, this dynamic reinforces control. Every touch, every sensation, every stolen moment of pleasure becomes a privilege, something they earn under your guidance. It's not just about teasing—it's about wielding the kind of power that keeps them coming back for more, desperate to please, desperate for you.

Required Tools & Preparation

- Toys for stimulation (vibrators, hands, etc.).
- Restraints (optional but highly effective).
- Timer for setting teasing intervals.

Execution

Step 1: Explain the Rules

Lay down the law: *"You're not allowed to finish until I say so. If you do, there will be consequences."*

Step 2: Tease to the Edge

Use a vibrator, your hands, or other tools to bring them close to climax. Stop just before they reach the point of no return. Pause, smile, and say, *"Not yet."*

Step 3: Repeat... and Repeat Again

The magic of edging is in the repetition. Each time they get closer, the denial becomes more torturous.

Step 4: Decide Their Fate

When you're satisfied with their frustration (and your own entertainment), either grant them release—or don't. You're in charge.

Punishment Spotlight

Set the stage with a wicked promise: they'll be edged five times before you even consider granting them release. Let that anticipation settle in, knowing you're about to take them on a tantalizing rollercoaster of frustration and desire. Start the game by guiding them right to the brink of climax—then stop. Hold them there, trembling and desperate, as you savor the power you have over their body. Make them count each edge aloud, their voice shaky with need as the numbers climb. When they finally reach the fifth edge, pause and let the moment hang in the air. Their body will be begging for mercy, their eyes pleading for release. But it's your call. Will you let them finish, or decide they need just a little more torment before they've truly earned it? The choice is yours, and the control is intoxicating.

Pro-Level Variations

Take edging to a whole new level by stretching their anticipation in ways they won't soon forget. Timed denial is a masterstroke of control—set a timer for how long they'll stay on the edge, whether it's hours, days, or even weeks. Let their longing build until it's all they can think about, making their eventual release feel like a hard-earned reward. For the daring, introduce public teasing. Add subtle stimulation during a discreet outing—a small toy, a knowing touch, or a whispered command—leaving them squirming while the world remains blissfully unaware of their predicament. Want to keep control from a distance? Use remote-controlled toys and orchestrate their torment wherever you are. The buzz of a button press, the look on their face as they try to hold it together—it's the ultimate power play, keeping them under your thumb no matter the distance.

Safety Tips

Play it safe, though. Keep denial within the bounds of consent, ensuring their frustration stays in the realm of tantalizing fun and never crosses into discomfort. Stay attuned to their reactions and check in frequently to keep the experience equal parts sexy, satisfying, and unforgettable

Aftercare

Denial can leave your submissive feeling vulnerable, so offer plenty of comfort and praise. Let them know their obedience was worth it—whether or not you let them finish.

The Point

Denial and edging are about teasing them to their limit while maintaining total control. It's a power trip you won't soon forget —and neither will they.

Chapter 13

Temperature Play – The Heat of the Moment (and the Chill of Control)

Temperature play is where fire meets ice—literally. By introducing hot and cold sensations, you keep your submissive guessing and on edge, amplifying their sensitivity and vulnerability. Whether it's a slow drip of wax or an icy trail down their spine, this punishment is both thrilling and artistic. It's about contrast: the searing heat of dominance and the icy chill of submission. And the best part? Watching them squirm as you decide what's next.

Why Temperature Play Works

Temperature play is an electrifying way to heighten sensations and captivate the senses. The contrast of extreme heat or cold ignites nerve endings, creating an intensity that's impossible to ignore. The element of surprise adds another layer, as the unpredictability of ice or wax keeps your submissive on edge—wondering what's coming next. And let's not forget the visual drama: the slow drip of wax, the glistening trail of melting ice, or the steam rising from warmed skin. It's a feast for the eyes as much as the body, leaving a lasting impression.

Required Tools & Preparation

- Ice Cubes: The easiest way to bring the chill.
- Massage Candles: Designed for safe, low-temperature wax play.
- Bowls of Warm/Cold Water: For soaking tools or hands.

Execution

Step 1: Prepare the Tools

Make sure everything is ready to go before you begin. Test wax temperature on yourself first to ensure it's safe, and have a towel or cloth nearby for cleanup.

Step 2: Tease the Sensations

Start with a light touch—run an ice cube along their arm or drip a tiny amount of wax on a non-sensitive area (like their shoulder). Gauge their reaction and adjust intensity as needed.

Step 3: Contrast the Temperatures

Switch between hot and cold to keep them guessing. For example: Drip warm wax on their chest, then follow it with an ice cube; Use a cold spoon on one side of their body while massaging the other with warm oil.

Step 4: Finish with a Grand Gesture

End with a dramatic flourish, like a slow wax drizzle down their spine or an ice cube melting on their stomach. Let the sensation linger before moving into aftercare.

Punishment Spotlight

To set the stage for temperature play, have your submissive lie down with their skin exposed, whether restrained for complete control or simply instructed to remain still. The anticipation begins as they wait, knowing the sensations you're about to bring will push them to focus entirely on you. Begin by lighting a massage candle, allowing the wax to melt into warm liquid. Drip it onto their skin in slow, deliberate strokes, each drop designed to tease and ignite their senses. Once their body has adjusted to the warmth, introduce the contrasting chill of an ice cube, tracing the same path the wax took. The sudden shift from heat to cold will leave their nerve endings buzzing. Alternate between the two, keeping them guessing and heightening their awareness of every change.

Pro-Level Variations

For added creativity, transform the wax into an art form. Draw shapes, write words, or leave teasing messages on their skin, blending control with playful flair. Blindfold them and use the ice to create unpredictable patterns, letting their mind race as their body responds. Incorporate tools dipped in warm or cold water to create even more variety in sensations, keeping them on edge with every touch.

Safety Tips

Safety is essential for temperature play to remain enjoyable and risk-free. Stick to massage candles specifically designed for wax play, as regular candles burn too hot and can cause harm. Always test wax and tools on your own skin first to ensure the temperature is safe, and focus on fleshy areas like the back, thighs, or chest to avoid overly sensitive spots. Keep a towel or bowl of water close for quick adjustments, ensuring the experience stays safe while being utterly tantalizing.

Aftercare

Temperature play can leave skin sensitive and your submissive emotionally heightened. Offer a warm blanket, soothing touch, and lots of praise for their endurance. Check in about how the sensations felt to ensure it was a positive experience.

The Point

Temperature play is all about contrast and control. Whether you're melting wax or trailing ice, this punishment is as creative as it is effective. It's hot, it's cold, and it's always unforgettable.

Chapter 14

The Clothing Rule – Dressing for Discipline

When you control what your submissive wears, you extend your power over their identity, choices, and comfort. Whether it's enforcing a strict dress code or choosing deliberately uncomfortable attire, the clothing rule turns an everyday necessity into a creative, constant reminder of your dominance.

Why The Clothing Rule Works

The clothing rule is the perfect blend of subtle dominance and playful creativity, ensuring your authority is felt with every step they take. Whether it's a specific outfit, an underlayer they're secretly wearing, or even a ridiculous pair of mismatched socks, the rule keeps them connected to you, a constant reminder of who's in control. This dynamic works equally well in public or private. Out in the world, it's a discreet display of power—only the two of you know what's beneath the surface. At home, it can be as bold or cheeky as you like, turning even the most mundane day into a game of submission and obedience. The beauty of the clothing rule lies in its endless possibilities. From sultry lingerie that fuels desire to playful quirks like deliberately mismatched outfits, it's a customizable tool that strengthens the dynamic while keeping things fresh and exciting. It's not just about what they wear—it's about how it makes them feel, and how it deepens the connection between you.

Required Tools & Preparation

A wardrobe or accessory you choose.

Execution

Step 1: Set the Rule

Make it clear: *"Today, you'll wear exactly what I tell you, and you'll keep it on until I say otherwise. No exceptions."*

Step 2: Choose the Outfit

The punishment can be tailored to suit your dynamic and the level of intensity you want to bring. For public outings, choose something embarrassing yet discreet, like mismatched shoes that make them self-conscious without drawing too much attention. If the goal is to create a physical challenge, opt for deliberately uncomfortable clothing, such as a tight corset or scratchy fabric that constantly reminds them of your control. Alternatively, select a specific item for them to wear, like your shirt, and instruct them to keep it on all day without offering any explanation. Each approach reinforces your authority while keeping the experience uniquely tied to your dynamic.

Step 3: Enforce Compliance

Throughout the day, check on their obedience. If they try to bend the rules, add consequences: *"Did I say you could take that off? That's another hour in it."*

Punishment Spotlight

Start by selecting an outfit for your submissive that pushes them out of their comfort zone—something they'd never choose on their own. It could be a bright, gaudy accessory, a pair of playful socks, or an outfit with clashing patterns that screams, *This was not my idea.* The key is making it just awkward enough to get under their skin while still being fun. Once the outfit is chosen, set the rule with unwavering authority: *"This is what you're wearing all day. Don't even think about changing it."* Watch the subtle shifts in their demeanor as they navigate their day in the attire you've dictated. The occasional blush or awkward glance is all part of the punishment. For an added twist, introduce challenges. Perhaps they have to take a picture of themselves in the outfit, or even casually show it to someone—always with discretion and mutual consent, of course. The goal is to keep them acutely aware of your control, even in the smallest, most unexpected ways. It's playful, effective, and undeniably yours to command.

Pro-Level Variations

Take the clothing rule to new heights with creative twists that keep them constantly aware of your control. Have them wear lingerie of your choosing beneath their everyday clothes, a secret reminder of your influence no one else will notice. For a subtle but undeniable mark of your authority, assign a specific accessory like a bracelet, scarf, or discreet collar they must wear in public. For a playful challenge, introduce themed dressing. Make them stick to a single color from head to toe, embrace an exaggeratedly childish look, or go overboard with formal attire that turns mundane errands into an event. These variations keep things fresh, fun, and deliciously dynamic, ensuring they never forget who's pulling the strings.

Safety Tips

When incorporating clothing punishments, always prioritize safety and comfort. Choose outfits that might challenge their confidence but never cause physical discomfort or restrict movement in a way that could be unsafe. Public punishments should remain discreet and fully consensual, ensuring no one outside your dynamic is unintentionally involved or made uncomfortable. The goal is to maintain trust and connection, keeping the experience enjoyable and respectful for both of you.

Aftercare

After the punishment ends, let them relax in their favorite comfortable clothing. Compliment their effort and obedience—it'll make them feel appreciated.

The Point

The clothing rule blends power, creativity, and a touch of humor, ensuring your authority is felt with every step they take.

Chapter 15

Corner Time with a Twist – The Art of Doing Nothing

Ah, corner time—the ultimate "think about what you've done" punishment. But why stop at just standing there? With a little creativity, you can turn this classic discipline into a mental and physical challenge that leaves your submissive humbled and obedient. It's simple, effective, and surprisingly versatile.

Why Corner Time Works

Corner time is deceptively simple but powerfully effective. It's a mental challenge that strips away distractions, forcing your submissive to sit with their thoughts—and your authority. Standing still and doing nothing might sound easy, but in practice, it's far from it. The stillness becomes its own form of discipline, heightening their awareness of the moment and their actions.

It's not just about the mind, either. Add specific positions, like kneeling or standing with arms raised, or small tasks to create a physical component. These subtle additions transform corner time into a full-body exercise in obedience and endurance.

Above all, corner time is a moment for reflection. Alone with their thoughts, your submissive is left to confront their behavior, the dynamic, and the power you hold over them. It's a simple but deeply effective way to reinforce authority while encouraging introspection and growth.

Required Tools & Preparation

- A quiet, distraction-free corner.
- Optional props: small objects to hold, post-it notes, or restraints.
- A timer to set the duration.

Execution

Step 1: Announce the Punishment

Calmly explain what's about to happen: *"You'll stand in that corner for 15 minutes, arms raised. Don't move until I say so."* Set clear expectations, including the consequences for failure.

Step 2: Add a Challenge

To make corner time more interesting, incorporate one of the following twists:

- Balancing Act: Have them hold an object (like a book) on their head or in their hands.
- Silent Reflection: No talking, sighing, or shifting allowed.
- Physical Positioning: Kneeling or standing on tiptoes adds a physical element.

Step 3: Monitor Compliance

Check in silently, walking behind them or observing their posture. The suspense of your presence (or absence) heightens their focus.

Step 4: Review the Outcome

Once the time is up, ask them to explain what they reflected on—or punish them further if they didn't follow the rules.

Punishment Spotlight

Set the scene by instructing your submissive to stand in the corner, arms raised above their head, each hand gripping a light object like a candle or small bottle. The simplicity of the task belies its challenge, as the minutes stretch and the strain begins to creep in. Once they're in position, start the timer and let the discipline begin. Slowly circle them, your presence a constant reminder of your control. Occasionally adjust their posture with a firm touch or tease them with a playful yet commanding comment: *"Already feeling the burn? I thought you were tougher than that."* The real fun comes when the timer resets—should their grip falter or an object drop, you calmly, deliberately start over. Their determination to succeed grows with each moment, turning this punishment into a mental and physical test of endurance that keeps them focused entirely on you.

Pro-Level Variations

Elevate corner time by introducing creative twists that amplify the challenge and deepen their focus. Blindfolding them removes visual distractions, forcing their attention inward and intensifying the psychological aspect of the punishment. For an added layer of reflection, have them write a short note or mantra, like *"I will obey"* or *"Patience is a virtue,"* and pin it on the wall in front of them. Each glance at their own words becomes a subtle reminder of why they're there. If you're feeling particularly mischievous, implement timed resets. For every slip—a dropped object, movement, or a word spoken without permission—the timer starts over. This transforms the punishment into a precise exercise in discipline and control, keeping them focused and mindful of their every action.

Safety Tips

Always prioritize their physical well-being. Avoid prolonged positions that could lead to strain, and ensure their posture is safe and sustainable. If the punishment extends beyond 15 minutes, allow for brief breaks to prevent discomfort. Remember, the goal is discipline and connection, not causing pain or harm, ensuring the experience remains intense yet consensual and enjoyable.

Aftercare

Corner time can feel emotionally intense, so offer reassurance once it's over. Praise their effort or discuss the lesson you wanted them to learn.

The Point

Corner time is the ultimate low-effort, high-impact punishment. By adding a creative twist, you turn it into a challenge that reinforces discipline, patience, and respect.

Chapter 16

Ice Play with a Punishing Twist

Ice play is the ultimate in sensory torture: cold, sharp, and utterly unforgettable. But this isn't just about making your submissive shiver—it's about turning temperature into a tool for control. Whether you're trailing an ice cube down their spine or making them hold it until it melts, this punishment is as versatile as it is chilling.

Ice play adds a unique edge to discipline, blending discomfort with heightened sensation for an experience they'll remember long after the ice has melted.

Why Ice Play Works

Ice play is a sensory experience that demands attention. The cold shocks nerve endings awake, delivering an intensity that can't be ignored. Each touch sends a jolt through the body, heightening awareness and drawing them deeper into the moment. It's not just physical—it's a mental challenge too. Holding or enduring the chill of ice requires focus and endurance, creating a balance of surrender and control that keeps them on edge. The combination of sensation and submission transforms a simple cube of ice into a powerful tool of dominance. What makes ice play truly unforgettable is the lasting impression it leaves. The contrast of cold against warm skin and the unmistakable control it represents become etched into memory, making every moment feel both exhilarating and deeply intimate.

Required Tools & Preparation

- Ice cubes, crushed ice, or an ice pack.
- Towels or a waterproof surface to avoid mess.

Execution

Step 1: Prepare the Submissive

Explain the punishment and set the rules: *"You will hold this ice cube until it melts completely. If you drop it, we start again—and trust me, I have plenty of ice."* Position them for maximum exposure: kneeling, standing, or lying down.

Step 2: Introduce the Ice

Begin with simple contact: Run the ice along their neck, back, or inner thighs. Place it directly in their hands or have them hold it against their skin.

Step 3: Add Challenges

Make the punishment more creative:

- Have them hold the ice between their knees or thighs without dropping it.
- Combine ice with sensory deprivation (e.g., blindfolds) for heightened reactions.

- Alternate between ice and a warm object for contrasting sensations.

Step 4: Push Their Limits

Encourage endurance but remain attentive to their comfort. Tease them with comments like, *"Is it cold? Good. That's the point."*

Punishment Spotlight

Start by setting the tone with a simple yet deviously effective challenge. Have your submissive kneel before you, their hands open and ready for instruction. Place a single ice cube in their palm, the chill immediately jolting their senses. With a commanding glance, instruct them to hold the ice perfectly still until it melts entirely. The seconds stretch into minutes as the cold seeps into their skin, testing their endurance and focus. Each tremble, each shiver is a sign of their effort to obey. Should they falter—dropping the ice or shifting their posture—your response is calm and deliberate. Replace the ice with an almost smug smile, resetting the task and watching as they redouble their efforts. The simplicity of the punishment only heightens its effectiveness, making it a mental and physical exercise in obedience that's impossible to forget.

Pro-Level Variations

Take ice play to the next level by turning it into an artful and sensual experience. Use an ice cube to "write" words, symbols, or teasing designs on their skin, each frosty touch leaving a trail of sensation and a visual reminder of your control. The combination of the cold and your deliberate movements turns their body into a canvas of submission. For a more intense experience, alternate the ice with contrasting temperatures. Follow the icy chill with the warm glide of your hand or a low-temperature candle, creating a push-pull of sensations that keeps their nerves on high alert. The rapid shifts between hot and cold amplify the intensity, leaving them breathless and at your mercy. If you're in the mood for a challenge, introduce timed holds. Have them grip multiple ice cubes, increasing the duration with each round as they strive to meet your demands. The growing difficulty tests their focus, endurance, and willingness to obey, making every second a testament to your authority. It's a game of control and surrender, where every shiver and gasp is yours to command.

Safety Tips

When incorporating ice play into your scenes, safety should always come first. Avoid keeping ice in prolonged contact with sensitive or thin-skinned areas, as this can lead to frostbite or unnecessary discomfort. Focus on fleshy areas like the palms, thighs, or back to ensure the cold remains stimulating without risk. Pay close attention to their physical reactions throughout the scene. Shivering, excessive redness, or signs of discomfort may indicate it's time to pause or adjust. Keep communication open, even if it's through non-verbal cues, to ensure the experience stays enjoyable and consensual. Have towels on hand to quickly dry off and warm them when the scene is over. A gentle touch and soothing warmth not only provide comfort but also create an intimate moment of care and connection after the intensity of the play.

Aftercare

After ice play, provide warmth—a soft blanket, a warm drink, or your touch. Reassure them with praise for their endurance and discuss how the punishment made them feel.

The Point

Ice play is a chilling reminder of your control. It's intense, intimate, and completely unforgettable—proof that even the simplest tools can deliver the coldest discipline.

Chapter 17

Forced Stillness – The Unmoving Ordeal

Sometimes, the most excruciating punishments aren't about pain but the struggle for control. Enter forced stillness, where every twitch, every fidget, and every breath becomes a battle. This punishment challenges your submissive's physical discipline and mental fortitude, turning their own body into their adversary. Forced stillness is elegant, torturous, and deceptively simple. It's a test of obedience that will leave them humbled and fully aware of your dominance.

Why Forced Stillness Works

Forced stillness is a deceptively simple but profoundly effective punishment that tests both the mind and body. Holding a position under your command becomes a mental challenge, requiring focus and discipline as they fight the urge to move. It's a battle of willpower, with every second stretching longer under the weight of your authority. Even the simplest pose—standing straight, kneeling, or holding their arms in place—turns grueling over time. Muscles ache, tremble, and beg for relief, making the physical strain an undeniable reminder of their submission. What makes it genuinely potent is the heightened awareness it creates. With your watchful eye fixed on them, every moment becomes magnified. The tiniest slip feels monumental, and their desire to please intensifies every passing second. It's a punishment that reinforces control, sharpens focus, and leaves a lasting impression of your dominance.

Required Tools & Preparation

A flat surface or a sturdy chair.

Execution

Step 1: Position Your Submissive

Choose a position that's challenging but safe for prolonged stillness. Examples: Standing with arms outstretched; Sitting perfectly upright without leaning; Kneeling with hands behind their back. Set the rules: *"You will hold this position for 10 minutes. If you move or complain, we start over."*

Step 2: Add Layers of Discipline

Make the punishment more intense by introducing additional challenges:

- Balance a book or light object on their head or hands.
- Place a small object between their knees and demand they hold it steady.
- Use your voice or tools (a feather, cane, or paddle) to keep them focused.

Step 3: Monitor and Correct

Stand over them, silently observing—or occasionally issuing

commands to adjust their posture. The suspense of your attention heightens their struggle.

Step 4: Escalate If Necessary

If they falter, calmly restart the timer or introduce a secondary punishment (e.g., a quick spanking or extra time added).

Punishment Spotlight

et the tone with a deceptively simple yet challenging task. Hand your submissive a small, unlit candle to hold in each hand, their arms extended while standing or kneeling. The task seems easy at first, but the strain will build quickly, testing their focus and endurance. Once they're in position, ensure their balance is steady and their posture perfect. The tension begins as the seconds tick by, every tremor a sign of their effort to obey. If a candle slips from their grasp, don't hesitate—restart the timer, or for an added twist, replace the fallen candle with a heavier object, ramping up the difficulty. Heighten the psychological challenge with a commanding whisper: *"Don't drop it. I'm watching every move."* Let your presence and words seep into their mind, making the task as much about control and concentration as physical strength. The intensity of your gaze will keep them trembling, desperate to prove themselves worthy under your watchful eye.

Pro-Level Variations

Take forced stillness to the next level with creative twists that heighten the challenge and amplify control. Blindfolding them removes their ability to anticipate, forcing them to focus entirely on their posture and the sensations around them. Without sight, every sound, every shift in the air becomes a distraction they must overcome. Introduce temperature play as a motivator. If they move or falter, press an ice cube to their skin or lightly graze them with a warm object to remind them of the stakes. The contrasting sensations keep them hyperaware and reinforce your dominance. For the ultimate test of obedience, add timed resets. Each time they move, complain, or lose their balance, increase the duration of the punishment. Knowing that every slip adds more time keeps them striving for absolute perfection.

Safety Tips

Prioritize their well-being by avoiding positions that could cause strain on joints or muscles, especially over extended periods. For beginners, keep sessions brief—five to ten minutes is a great starting point to build their endurance. Throughout the scene, monitor their physical state closely, ensuring the challenge remains intense without crossing into pain or discomfort. The goal is to push their limits safely while keeping the experience rewarding for both of you.

Aftercare

After the ordeal, massage or stretch any areas that were strained. Offer verbal reassurance and praise their endurance. This punishment is a mental and physical challenge, so support them as they come down from the experience.

The Point

Forced stillness is a lesson in patience, focus, and submission. It's subtle yet excruciating, reminding them that sometimes the hardest thing to do is nothing at all.

Chapter 18

The Humiliation Box – A Lesson in Vulnerability

Few punishments are as psychologically intense as humiliation. The Humiliation Box is a customizable punishment where your submissive faces tasks, challenges, or restrictions designed to push their ego aside and reinforce their role. Whether it's wearing a silly item, reciting embarrassing phrases, or completing a demeaning chore, this punishment leaves them humbled and obedient.

Why Humiliation Works

Humiliation taps into the mind like few other tools can, forcing your submissive to confront their role and embrace it fully. It's a raw form of mental submission, stripping away pretenses and leaving them exposed, obedient, and completely yours. At its core, humiliation deepens trust. Allowing themselves to be vulnerable in this way requires a level of intimacy that strengthens the bond between you. Each blush, stammer, or nervous laugh becomes a testament to the connection and safety they feel in your hands. The beauty of humiliation lies in its endless creativity. Whether it's playful teasing, embarrassing tasks, or subtle public challenges, you can shape the experience to fit your dynamic perfectly. It's not about cruelty—it's about exploring vulnerability, deepening your connection, and having a little wicked fun along the way.

Required Tools & Preparation

- Props: silly hats, costumes, or accessories.
- Tasks: writing lines, singing songs, or cleaning chores.
- Optional: a literal box filled with "humiliation tasks" they must draw from.

Execution

Announce their punishment with authority: *"Since you broke the rules, you'll complete three tasks from the Humiliation Box. Each one must be done exactly as I say."*

Step 2: Present the Tasks

Hand them a box containing slips of paper with pre-written tasks or select challenges yourself. Examples: Wear a ridiculous outfit and pose for a picture or Write "I'm a naughty submissive" 50 times.

Step 3: Monitor Their Progress

Watch as they complete each task. Correct them if they falter, and don't forget to tease: *"Oh, you think that's embarrassing? Just wait until the next one."*

Step 4: Wrap It Up

Once all tasks are completed, decide if they've earned redemption—or if they need to revisit the box.

Punishment Spotlight

Set the scene with a playful yet mortifying task: hand your submissive a sheet of paper and a box of crayons, instructing them to draw a self-portrait of themselves "in trouble." The simplicity of the assignment belies its power to push their buttons, making them feel deliciously vulnerable under your watchful eye. Once they're seated and ready, set a timer for ten minutes. Sit back and enjoy the show as they squirm, cheeks flushed, and struggle to produce something remotely presentable. Their every hesitation, every awkward scribble, becomes part of the punishment. When the timer goes off, take their masterpiece in hand and review it with dramatic flair. Comment with exaggerated critiques like, *"Is this supposed to be you? Stick figures? I think you can do better."* Let your tone stay teasing but firm, driving home their embarrassment without crossing into cruelty.

Safety Tips

Ensure the task remains within the bounds of playful humiliation, avoiding anything that might touch on sensitive emotional or psychological areas. Humiliation should always be consensual, a shared game of submission and trust, not harm. The goal is to challenge their pride while keeping the experience lighthearted and reinforcing your dynamic.

The Point

The Humiliation Box is a playful but powerful way to remind them who's in charge while fostering deeper trust and vulnerability.

Chapter 19

Weighted Patience – Bearing the Burden

Weighted Patience transforms submission into a physical and mental challenge. By adding literal weight to their punishment, you create an ordeal that pushes their endurance and focus to the limit. Each second under the burden is a reminder of your control, and every slip tests their commitment. Whether it's holding still, balancing precariously, or bearing weight in an awkward position, this punishment is as symbolic as it is demanding.

Why Weighted Patience Works

Weighted patience is a punishment that engages both the body and mind, creating a powerful display of control and endurance. The physical challenge of holding a weight for an extended period tests their strength and stamina, reminding them of their submission with every tremble and strain. The act carries symbolic power. The weight isn't just a physical object—it represents their role, their responsibilities, and the balance of your dynamic. Each second they endure becomes a testament to their commitment to you and the relationship you've built together. Beyond the physical, it's a mental exercise in fortitude. Staying perfectly still under pressure demands focus, concentration, and resilience. Every moment becomes a battle of will, sharpening their discipline while reinforcing your authority. Weighted patience is more than a punishment—it's a lesson in strength, devotion, and unwavering submission.

Required Tools & Preparation

- Weights: Dumbbells, sandbags, books, or household objects.
- Sturdy props: Chairs, tables, or kneeling pads.
- A timer to track the duration.
- Optional: Additional challenges like blindfolds, sensory play, or verbal commands.

Execution

Step 1: Positioning the Submissive

Choose a pose that combines stability with a sense of vulnerability. Examples: Standing Hold: Submissive stands with arms extended, holding weights or Kneeling Balance: Place a weight on their back as they kneel. Set clear rules: *"You will hold this position without moving for five minutes. Any slip or complaint adds more weight—or more time."*

Step 2: Start with the Basics

Begin with manageable weight and a short timer to gauge their endurance. Observe their posture and adjust as needed to ensure safety and maximum challenge.

Step 3: Add Layers of Difficulty

Once they're comfortable (or not-so-comfortable), escalate:

- Increased Weight: Gradually add more weight or replace lighter items with heavier ones.
- Extended Duration: Start with a short time limit and increase with each success—or failure.
- Dual Challenges: Combine the weight with verbal tasks (e.g., reciting a mantra) or sensory deprivation.

Step 4: Monitor and Correct

Stand nearby and observe their performance. Use verbal cues to tease and correct their form: *"Your arms are drooping. Do you want me to add more weight?"*, *"You're shaking already? We've only just begun."*

Punishment Spotlight

Set the stage for a test of endurance and obedience by having your submissive kneel in position, a sandbag balanced across their shoulders. Their hands, resting palms-up, hold light weights that seem to grow heavier with every passing second. The setup is simple but demanding, creating an immediate focus on submission and control. Once they're in place, command them to stay perfectly still for five minutes. As they hold the position, slowly circle them, your presence a constant reminder of your authority. Inspect their form with an exacting gaze, and every so often, tap the sandbag gently to test their steadiness, letting them feel the weight of your scrutiny as much as the physical load. If they falter—shifting position, dropping a weight, or losing balance—don't let it slide. Reset the timer with a calm, deliberate smile, or increase the challenge by adding another bag. The punishment becomes as much a mental challenge as a physical one, pushing their limits while keeping them keenly aware of your control.

Pro-Level Variations

Take weighted patience to the next level by introducing dynamic balance. Challenge your submissive to carefully move, such as crawling with a book balanced on their back, demanding both focus and precision. Every step becomes a test of their ability to maintain composure under pressure. Add a sensory twist by combining weights with temperature play. Have them hold warm or cold objects in their palms while staying perfectly still, amplifying the physical and mental challenge. The shifting sensations keep them on edge, heightening their awareness of every moment. For those ready to explore a touch of public discretion, assign a weighted pose in a subtle setting. Perhaps a long stance with a bag casually draped over their shoulder or holding an object in a specific way while you're out together. The subtle humiliation of knowing they're performing for your eyes alone, even in public, deepens their submission and connection to you.

Safety Tips

When incorporating weighted patience into your dynamic, prioritize your submissive's well-being at every step. Choose weights that challenge without risking strain or injury—this is about control and endurance, not physical harm. Pay close attention to their posture, ensuring it remains stable and safe throughout the scene. Proper alignment is key, especially for longer durations, to prevent discomfort or undue stress on joints and muscles. Monitor them closely as they perform the task, watching for signs of overexertion like shaking, excessive fatigue, or difficulty breathing. Stay communicative, even if only through agreed-upon gestures, to ensure the punishment remains intense but always consensual and safe. The goal is discipline, connection, and growth—not harm.

Aftercare

Massage or stretch areas that experienced strain to prevent stiffness or soreness. Praise their effort and endurance, emphasizing how they've demonstrated their submission under pressure.

The Point

Weighted Patience is a symbolic and physical test of their role, turning submission into a tangible, memorable experience. It's a punishment they'll feel long after the weight is lifted.

Chapter 20

Obstacle Crawl – Earning Forgiveness

The Obstacle Crawl combines physical effort with mental submission, challenging your submissive to navigate a series of tasks or hurdles. Whether they're crawling under furniture, balancing objects, or pausing for specific tasks, this punishment is as creative as it is grueling. It's a full-body expression of their willingness to endure and obey.

Why Obstacle Crawls Work

Obstacle crawls are a powerful combination of physical and symbolic submission. The act of crawling forces your submissive into a position that visually and tactilely reinforces their role, reminding them of their place in the dynamic with every movement. What makes this punishment especially engaging is its creative potential. You can design the course to perfectly suit your needs, whether it's a simple crawl across the room or a more elaborate path filled with challenges and surprises. Each obstacle becomes an opportunity to deepen their focus and test their obedience. On a deeper level, crawling represents humility and devotion. By moving on their hands and knees, they embody their submission in a raw, symbolic way that highlights their willingness to obey and surrender to you completely. It's a punishment that goes beyond physicality, creating a lasting impression of trust and control.

Required Tools & Preparation

- Household items to create obstacles (e.g., pillows, chairs, ropes).
- Props for tasks (e.g., toys to fetch, bowls to balance).
- Optional: Blindfolds or restraints for added difficulty.

Execution

Step 1: Design the Course

Create a path with obstacles that require effort and focus, such as: Crawling under chairs or through rope barriers or Balancing items (e.g., a spoon or small object) while moving.

Step 2: Explain the Challenge

Set clear expectations: *"You will crawl through this course without hesitation. If you fail, we start over—and I'll make it harder."*

Step 3: Monitor Their Progress

Follow closely, watching for mistakes or hesitation. Add pressure by teasing them with comments like, *"Are you slowing down already? Keep moving."*

Step 4: Enforce Consequences

If they drop an object, falter, or fail a task, impose a penalty: Restart the course. Add an additional obstacle or challenge. Assign an immediate physical punishment, like a spanking.

Punishment Spotlight

Transform a simple room into a field of submission by setting up an obstacle crawl. Scatter small objects—like toys, pieces of clothing, or other lightweight items—at various points along the space, creating a course they must navigate. Once everything is in place, command your submissive to fetch each object one at a time and bring it back to you. Make it clear that they are to crawl the entire time, maintaining proper posture as they move. The challenge isn't just physical—it's about focus and precision, ensuring they follow your instructions perfectly. If they falter—dropping an item, breaking form, or hesitating—don't let the mistake go unnoticed. Reset the task, calmly yet firmly, reminding them of your expectations. Each restart deepens their awareness of their role and reinforces the importance of obedience. It's not just a physical punishment—it's a symbolic act of devotion, each retrieved item a small tribute to your authority.

Pro-Level Variations

Add complexity and intensity to obstacle crawls with creative twists that push their limits. A blindfolded crawl heightens the challenge by removing their sight, forcing them to rely on touch, intuition, and your guidance. Every movement becomes more deliberate, and their submission deepens as they navigate the unknown. Introduce timed challenges to up the pressure. Set a strict time limit for completing the course, and watch as they scramble to balance speed with precision, knowing that failure means starting over or additional tasks. The ticking clock becomes another layer of control, keeping them focused and determined to meet your expectations. For a more daring variation, incorporate a subtle public element. Assign a discreet task in a public space, like fetching an object or completing a small action under your command. The thrill of submission combined with the need to stay unnoticed adds a delicious tension to the punishment.

Safety Tips

Always ensure the course is free of sharp or hazardous objects that could cause harm. Adjust the difficulty based on their physical ability, ensuring the tasks remain challenging yet achievable. The goal is to push their boundaries safely, keeping the experience intense but never overwhelming.

Aftercare

Help them clean up or guide them back to a comfortable position. Offer praise for their effort, and discuss how the task reinforced their obedience and focus.

The Point

The Obstacle Crawl is an engaging, full-body punishment that emphasizes effort, humility, and obedience. It's a creative way to challenge their submission and leave a lasting impression.

Chapter 21

Sensory Chaos – The Overload Ordeal

Sensory Chaos is the ultimate punishment for a submissive who thrives on control—or lack of it. By bombarding them with a mixture of intense sensations, you push them to the brink of their limits. Whether it's sudden sounds, contrasting temperatures, or rapid changes in stimulation, this punishment is about overwhelming their senses to reinforce your dominance. Sensory Chaos isn't just about physical overload—it's a mental battle that leaves them entirely at your mercy.

Why Sensory Chaos Works

Sensory chaos is the ultimate exercise in domination, placing you in total control of every sensation they experience. By overwhelming their senses with unpredictable stimuli, you leave them unable to anticipate what's coming next. This keeps their mind and body completely attuned to your commands, reinforcing your authority. The flood of sensations heightens their sensitivity, amplifying even the smallest touch, sound, or movement. Each shift in stimuli becomes sharper, more intense, and impossible to ignore, drawing them deeper into the moment. On a psychological level, sensory chaos delivers a profound mental impact. The inability to predict or adapt forces them to surrender control entirely, leaving them vulnerable and dependent on you. This surrender builds trust, strengthens submission, and creates a connection rooted in absolute dominance and mutual consent. It's a rollercoaster of intensity that leaves a lasting impression on both body and mind.

Required Tools & Preparation

- Sensory tools: feathers, floggers, vibrators, ice cubes, warm objects.
- Noise-makers: bells, headphones, or even your voice.
- Optional: Blindfolds, earmuffs, or restraints to isolate or enhance senses.

Execution

Step 1: Restrict Their Awareness

Start by blindfolding or partially restraining them. Explain the punishment: *"You're going to feel everything I decide, exactly how and when I want. You don't get to prepare—you just get to endure."*

Step 2: Introduce Contrasting Sensations

Bombard their senses in rapid succession or simultaneous bursts. Examples: Trail ice down their back while flogging their thighs. Whisper in one ear while creating a sudden loud noise in the other. Alternate between soft touches and sharp pinches.

Step 3: Keep Them Guessing

Change the rhythm and intensity unpredictably to keep

them off balance. Pause suddenly, letting them stew in anticipation before resuming. Tease them with comments like, *"Is it too much? It's only just begun."*

Step 4: Push and Release

When they're nearing their breaking point, slow down and let them catch their breath—before ramping back up for one final round of chaos.

Punishment Spotlight

Turn their world into a storm of sensation. With ice cubes in one hand and a warm object—like a heated towel or melted wax—in the other, blindfold your submissive and have them kneel or lie down, exposed and vulnerable to your every whim. Start the torment by alternating between the freezing chill of ice and the sultry heat of warmth on their skin. Move unpredictably, dragging an ice cube down their spine one moment and pressing heat against their thigh the next. Pause just long enough to make them squirm, anticipation thick in the air as they wonder what's coming. Command their focus with sharp, teasing words: *"Tell me where you feel it. Is it fire or ice?"* Their shaky voice, their gasps as the sensations collide—it's all yours, a symphony of control and surrender. Every touch becomes electric, every second a reminder that you're the one holding all the power. This isn't just punishment—it's a game of domination and desire that leaves them aching for more.

Pro-Level Variations

Take sensory chaos to a thrilling new level with advanced twists that intensify the experience. Strip away all sound by using only physical sensations—no words, no cues—forcing them to rely entirely on the unpredictability of your touch. The silence will magnify every shiver, every gasp, as their body reacts without the comfort of context. For an even more electrifying scene, bring in a trusted partner to deliver simultaneous sensations. Imagine the chill of ice trailing down one side of their body while warm wax drips on the other, leaving them completely surrounded and overwhelmed. The dynamic becomes a tantalizing dance of confusion and surrender. If you crave precision, introduce timed chaos. Set a timer and promise no relief until it rings. They'll writhe under the onslaught, knowing they're yours to tease and torment until every second ticks away.

Safety Tips

Keep the experience intense but never overwhelming. Take breaks to monitor their reactions and ensure they're processing the sensations comfortably. Always use tools and temperatures that are safe for skin contact, avoiding anything too extreme. Before and after, communicate openly to ensure the intensity matches their limits and desires, keeping the connection strong and consensual.

Aftercare

Offer warmth, soothing touches, and quiet reassurance. Discuss how the experience felt for both of you, focusing on how they endured and submitted to the chaos.

The Point

Sensory Chaos is a punishing reminder of your control over their body and mind. It's intense, intimate, and leaves no doubt about who holds the reins.

Chapter 22

Controlled Bruising – Marking the Moment

For some dynamics, nothing solidifies an act of dominance like a visible reminder. Controlled Bruising is a punishment that leaves its mark—literally. Whether it's from a paddle, cane, or flogger, the art of creating intentional, safe bruises is about precision, symbolism, and the lasting power of your authority. Each bruise tells a story, reminding them of the rules they broke and the submission they've offered.

Why Controlled Bruising Works

Controlled bruising is a potent expression of dominance, leaving a physical reminder that lingers long after the scene ends. Every mark becomes a silent, lasting symbol of your control—a visible testament to the dynamic you share. Psychologically, the act of marking deepens their submission. It's an intimate exchange, reinforcing trust as they allow you to leave your imprint on their body. Each bruise becomes a badge of surrender, a reminder of the power they've entrusted to you. Beyond the physical and mental connection, there's an artistic element to controlled bruising. Every mark tells a story, creating a visual representation of your shared experience. The patterns, colors, and placement reflect the intensity of your bond, turning their skin into a canvas of submission and devotion. It's not just discipline—it's art.

Required Tools & Preparation

- Impact tools: paddles, floggers, canes, or hands.
- A clean, safe surface for punishment.
- Ice packs or lotion for aftercare.

Execution

Step 1: Choose the Area

Select a part of their body that is safe for impact and appropriate for marking. Ideal areas include: Buttocks (soft and resilient). Thighs (more sensitive, but safe with proper technique). Shoulders or upper back (less common, but effective). Avoid sensitive or bony areas such as the spine, joints, or lower back.

Step 2: Set Expectations

Explain the punishment and what they can expect: *"You've earned this mark. I will bruise you as a reminder of your disobedience. It will fade, but the lesson will stay."* Discuss boundaries, including intensity and placement, to ensure trust.

Step 3: Execute with Precision

Use deliberate, controlled strikes to create bruises safely.

- Warm-Up: Begin with lighter strikes to prepare the skin.

- Build Intensity: Gradually increase force, observing their reactions.
- Targeted Strikes: Focus on specific spots to create uniform marks.

Use verbal cues to maintain control:

"You're doing well. Just a few more." "Stay still, or I'll add another."

Step 4: Admire and Reflect

Once the punishment is complete, inspect your work. Run your fingers over the bruises, offering praise or reminders of their significance.

Punishment Spotlight

Select a paddle or flogger featuring a unique design—perhaps with holes, ridges, or a textured surface—to create a striking, lasting pattern. Position your submissive securely, ensuring both stability and comfort. With precision and control, deliver measured strikes, allowing the distinctive design to imprint on their skin. Once the pattern emerges, run your fingers gently along the marks, tracing their contours and deepening the significance of the moment.

Pro-Level Variations

Symbolic Marks Craft intentional designs such as initials, meaningful symbols, or shapes that represent your unique dynamic, leaving a signature touch.

Layered Bruising Elevate the experience by alternating tools to create a tapestry of textures and depths on the skin for a multidimensional effect.

Paired Sensory Play Enhance the contrast by following each strike with a tender caress, gentle strokes, or the soothing application of lotion to amplify both sensation and intimacy.

Safety Tips

Always use proper impact techniques, ensuring strikes are controlled and avoiding excessive force. Stay attentive to their reactions, maintaining open communication to ensure they remain comfortable and consenting throughout. Afterward, provide thoughtful aftercare to soothe the skin and nurture trust, strengthening the bond between you.

Aftercare

Apply ice packs or lotion to the bruised area to reduce discomfort. Offer verbal reassurance, reminding them of the significance of the punishment and your care for their well-being.

The Point

Controlled Bruising is about precision, artistry, and creating a lasting impression—both physically and emotionally. It's a powerful way to mark your dominance while deepening your connection.

Chapter 23

Role Reversal – The Switch Punishment

Sometimes the best punishment is making your submissive experience your perspective. Role Reversal flips the dynamic, temporarily placing them in the Dominant role. It's a playful, humbling punishment that teaches empathy and reinforces why they trust your control. By putting them in charge, you reveal just how much responsibility and skill goes into your role—while keeping the power dynamic firmly in place.

Why Role Reversal Works

Role reversal flips the script, offering a fresh and often humbling perspective. By stepping into the role of authority, your submissive gains firsthand experience of the challenges and decisions that come with control. It's a powerful shift that deepens their understanding of your dynamic. The playful humiliation of fumbling through commands or struggling to maintain composure adds another layer of fun. Watching them attempt to take charge—and inevitably falling short—reinforces your superiority while keeping the experience light and engaging. Beyond the humor and perspective, role reversal adds depth to your relationship. It's a chance to explore new sides of your dynamic, bringing variety and a deeper connection to your shared journey. It's not just a game—it's a way to grow together.

Required Tools & Preparation

- Props: A symbolic "Dominant's item" (e.g., a collar or crop) to hand over temporarily.
- A clear script or list of tasks for them to perform.

Execution

Step 1: Announce the Reversal

Explain the punishment with authority: *"You think my role is easy? Let's see how you handle being in charge. But remember—this is still my game."* Hand them a prop to symbolize their temporary "power," but remind them it's an illusion.

Step 2: Set Their Tasks

Provide specific instructions for how they should act as the Dominant. Examples: Give commands (e.g., instructing you to hold a pose or perform a task). Use tools (e.g., delivering light impact play).

Step 3: Observe and Critique

Follow their lead while subtly maintaining control. Correct their mistakes with playful humiliation: *"Is that your idea of a command? "You call that a strike? Let me show you how it's done."*

Step 4: Reclaim Control

Once their "session" is complete, reassert your dominance: *"See? This is why you belong on your knees—not in my chair."*

Punishment Spotlight

Turn the tables and challenge your submissive to step into your shoes, instructing them to give you five commands as the Dominant. The setup is simple, but the task is designed to test their confidence and highlight the intricacies of control. As they issue commands, follow their instructions with an amused yet critical edge. Comment on their delivery—too soft, too hesitant, or maybe a bit unsure—and let them feel the pressure of getting it just right. Each stumble or moment of hesitation reinforces the difficulty of wielding authority, driving home their appreciation for your role. If they falter, hesitate, or fail to deliver effectively, introduce penalties. Reset the task or add an extra layer of punishment to remind them that dominance is earned, not faked. The experience becomes a playful but impactful lesson, reinforcing the balance of your dynamic while keeping the energy spicy and engaging.

Pro-Level Variations

Take role reversal to new heights with advanced twists that amplify the challenge and fun. In discreet public settings, allow them to briefly "lead," giving subtle commands or taking charge of a minor task. The thrill of public play combined with the weight of responsibility adds an extra layer of excitement. Introduce task reversal by assigning them duties you typically handle, such as setting up the scene, choosing tools, or establishing the mood. Watching them navigate these responsibilities will deepen their appreciation for the work you put into your role. End the session with a performance review, critiquing their "dominance" with playful seriousness. Assign a score and, if they fall short, enforce consequences that reestablish your control, turning their failure into another opportunity for submission.

Safety Tips

Keep role reversal playful and within clear, agreed-upon boundaries to ensure it remains a temporary exploration and doesn't disrupt your established dynamic. Avoid assigning tasks that could create long-term shifts in power unless both partners desire that evolution. Throughout the experience, ensure your submissive feels safe, supported, and free to laugh at their own stumbles—because this is as much about connection as it is about creativity.

Aftercare

Discuss how the reversal felt for both of you. Reaffirm the power dynamic by reminding them of their role and why they trust your leadership. Offer physical and verbal reassurance to bring them back to their comfort zone.

The Point

Role Reversal is a creative, humbling punishment that reinforces the importance of their submission while letting them peek behind the curtain of your authority. It's a reminder of why they belong on the receiving end of your power.

Chapter 24

The Silent Countdown – A Game of Anticipation

Silence can be deafening, especially when paired with anticipation. The Silent Countdown is a punishment that forces your submissive to endure the mental torment of waiting for the inevitable. Without verbal cues or a visible timer, they're left guessing when the next strike, command, or sensation will come. It's a test of patience, control, and their ability to stay in the moment.

Why Silent Countdown Works

The silent countdown is a beautifully tormenting psychological tool, plunging them into a state of uncertainty where every second feels like an eternity. The lack of verbal or visual cues creates a mental tension that amplifies their focus and submission, leaving them hanging on your every move with a mix of anxiety and desire. Anticipation becomes a weapon in your hands. They're desperate for a sign, a hint, anything to clue them in on what's coming next. The suspense keeps them fully engaged, their senses heightened as they wait, yearning for resolution. At its core, the silent countdown reinforces patience.

With no idea of what's next, they're forced to remain still, obedient, and fully present in the moment. It's a masterstroke of control that transforms waiting into an exercise in submission, trust, and the thrill of the unknown.

Required Tools & Preparation

- Impact tools (e.g., flogger, paddle, or bare hands).
- A timer you can conceal.

Execution

Step 1: Set the Rules

Position your submissive and explain the punishment: *"You'll stay perfectly still and silent. Each time you move or speak, the countdown resets—and trust me, you don't know when it ends."* Add sensory deprivation (e.g., a blindfold) for heightened suspense.

Step 2: Start the Countdown

Begin with a long pause to let the silence sink in. Then, deliver a sudden action:

- A strike with a paddle.
- A whispered command or tease.
- A feather or ice cube trailing over their skin.

Between actions, reset the silence. Let them stew in the uncertainty of when the next move will come.

Step 3: Escalate the Challenge

Increase the intensity of the actions or lengthen the silences to push their patience. If they move or speak, restart the countdown with a smirk: *"Oh, you couldn't wait? Let's try that again."*

Step 4: Decide When It Ends

After a set number of actions (or when you're satisfied with their obedience), bring the punishment to a close with a final strike or command.

Punishment Spotlight

Set the stage for a punishment that's as much about the waiting as it is about the strikes themselves. Begin by telling your submissive they'll receive five strikes—but leave them in the dark about when they'll happen. This setup alone is enough to ignite a delicious tension. Once they're blindfolded, make them wait, fully exposed to your control. Deliver each strike at unpredictable intervals, varying the intensity to keep them guessing. Let the pauses stretch just long enough to make them squirm with anticipation, their senses straining for any hint of your next move. When the final strike lands, lean in close and whisper, *"Good. You made it."* The soft affirmation contrasts with the sharp discipline, reinforcing your control while offering a moment of connection.

Pro-Level Variations

For an even more intense experience, extend the waits between strikes. Let the silence drag on, leaving them teetering between expectation and suspense. If you prefer precision, use a silent timer to structure the punishment while keeping them unaware of its rhythm, heightening the psychological tension. To deepen the sensory impact, alternate the strikes with softer sensations—a gentle feather trailing over their skin, the warmth of your breath against their neck. The interplay between sharp and soft keeps their body and mind in a state of heightened awareness, fully immersed in the moment and utterly yours.

Safety Tips

Monitor their physical and mental state—prolonged silence can be intense. Use clear boundaries to ensure they feel safe and supported.

Aftercare

Once the punishment ends, reassure them and discuss how the waiting felt. Provide physical comfort and praise for their patience.

The Point

The Silent Countdown is about making them focus on your control, building suspense and submission with every passing second of silence.

The Final Lesson – Dominance, Submission, and the Art of Connection

As we close this guide, let's strip things down to the raw, beating heart of BDSM punishments: the connection between Dominant and submissive. Every punishment you've tried, every rule enforced, every delicious boundary pushed—it all leads to one ultimate purpose. It's not just about discipline or obedience; it's about trust so deep it becomes unshakable, a dynamic so charged it leaves both of you breathless, and moments so unforgettable they linger long after the marks fade.

The truth is, the final lesson isn't about a specific punishment or technique. It's about the dance of dominance and submission, the mutual gift you give each other every time you step into your roles. Dominance is a gift of guidance, protection, and unwavering control. Submission is a gift of vulnerability, surrender, and profound trust. Together, these acts create a bond that is entirely unique—crafted by your hands, fueled by your desires, and alive with your connection.

So why does connection reign supreme? Because without trust, even the most wickedly creative punishment feels hollow. It's the intimacy of knowing your submissive inside and out—their limits, their triggers, their deepest needs—that transforms discipline into something powerful and meaningful. And when done right, a punishment doesn't just sting in the moment; it lingers in memory for its intensity, its purpose, and the way it brought you closer together.

Let's leave you with a ritual to bring it all full circle: The Ritual of Reconnection. Imagine this. The room is dimly lit, soft music hums in the background, and the world outside fades into nothingness. This isn't just about punishment—it's about focus. It's about them, about you, about the dynamic that pulses between you like a living thing.

Picture your submissive kneeling before you, their posture radiating respect and vulnerability. Maybe you tie a wrist with deliberate precision, fasten their collar, or rest a hand firmly on their shoulder. That small, symbolic act says everything: *This is our moment. This is who we are.*

Then, together, you reflect. Look them in the eye. Talk about how they've grown, how they've struggled, and where they've succeeded. If there's still a lesson left to be taught, deliver it now. A few measured spanks to emphasize a point, a sharp command to remind them of their place, or even a charged moment of enforced silence—whatever feels right for your unique bond.

When the punishment is done, don't just leave it hanging. Seal it with connection. Maybe it's a whispered affirmation that drips with meaning: *You are mine.* Maybe it's a firm touch, a long gaze, or a lingering kiss that pulls them back into the safety of your care. In that moment, everything—the struggle, the surrender, the lessons—is wrapped up in the intimacy of your shared power.

This book may be ending, but your journey is just beginning. Every punishment, every act of discipline, is a step deeper into the dynamic you're building together. Don't shy away from creativity—find new ways to challenge them, to surprise them,

The Final Lesson – Dominance, Submission, and the Art of Connec...

to keep the flame alive. Never stop communicating; your connection will only grow stronger as you adapt and evolve together. And above all, keep anchoring every punishment, every rule, every moment in the unshakable foundation of trust and love.

Here's your final command: take everything you've learned here and make it your own. These pages are just a starting point—a framework for the dynamic only you can bring to life. Play with it. Break it. Rebuild it. Make it a story that belongs to you both, filled with moments of passion, challenge, and triumph.

Dominance isn't about perfection, and submission isn't about weakness. It's about the power you create together: one act, one punishment, one connection at a time. Now go forth and write the next chapter of your story.

To every Dominant and submissive reading this: thank you for letting me be part of your journey. Your dynamic is yours alone, and that makes it extraordinary. This isn't just about punishments—it's about building a bond so deep, so intimate, and so fiercely unique that it becomes a masterpiece only you could create.

The rest is in your hands.

Clare and Anderson An Evening to Remember

The low purr of Anderson's car engine stilled as he pulled into the driveway, leaving behind the relentless chaos of the corporate battlefield. Inside, the house was a sanctuary of warmth and quiet, a stark contrast to the whirlwind of endless meetings, impossible decisions, and the constant pressure of being at the top. Loosening his tie and shrugging off his jacket, Anderson felt the day's weight begin to dissipate.

This wasn't just home—it was *her*. Clare. His anchor, his solace, the intoxicating calm in his storm. Just the thought of her was enough to shift his mood from weary to wicked.

"Clare?" His voice cut through the silence, low and commanding, a single word that held more power than a boardroom full of executives.

"Upstairs, Sir." The soft, submissive melody of her reply floated down, tinged with that spark of anticipation he loved.

A slow, predatory smile curved his lips as he climbed the stairs, each step a deliberate prolonging of the anticipation thrumming in his chest. The bedroom door stood ajar, spilling a crack of golden light into the hallway like a promise. Pushing it open, Anderson stopped just inside, his gaze locking onto the vision before him.

Clare knelt in the center of the room, poised with flawless grace. Her back was straight, hands resting lightly on her thighs, her head bowed just enough to radiate submission while letting him glimpse the delicate curve of her lips. She wore a sheer black drape that barely skimmed her curves, her collar glinting in the soft light like a declaration of belonging.

His.

Anderson prowled toward her, the sound of his polished shoes a steady counterpoint to her shallow, expectant breaths. He circled her like a wolf admiring its prey, savoring every detail—the slight tremble in her shoulders, the way her skin flushed under his gaze, the faint scent of lavender she'd so carefully chosen.

Behind her, he placed a hand on the nape of her neck, warm and firm. She shivered under his touch. "Did you wait long?" he asked, his voice a slow caress that made her toes curl.

"No, Sir," she whispered, though her tone betrayed just how much she'd been anticipating this.

"Good."

He moved in front of her, tilting her chin upward with a single finger. Her eyes met his, wide and brimming with trust, a quiet plea shimmering just beneath the surface.

"I've had a long day," he murmured, his thumb grazing the soft curve of her jaw. "And all I've been thinking about is this. You. Do you know why?"

Her voice was steady but laced with longing. "Because I'm yours, Sir."

"Exactly." His lips brushed her ear, and she gasped at the heat of his breath. "You're mine. My anchor. My peace."

Her breath hitched as he pulled back, his eyes dark and intent. "Stand."

Clare rose fluidly, the sheer fabric parting to reveal hints of lace beneath. Anderson's gaze roamed over her, hungry and possessive. "Take it off."

Her fingers made quick work of the tie at her waist, the robe slipping from her shoulders in a silken whisper. Beneath, she wore a black lace bodysuit that was both daring and exquisite, framing her body like art. Anderson let out a low, appreciative hum, stepping closer to let his hands trace her waist, her hips.

"Turn around," he commanded, his voice a velvet growl.

Clare obeyed, pivoting slowly. He drank in the sight of her—every curve, every line, the way the lace clung to her skin like it had been designed just for her. When she faced him again, his expression left no doubt about what was coming.

"Kneel. On the bed. Face the headboard."

She climbed onto the bed with quiet grace, positioning herself exactly as he'd instructed. Anderson moved to the dresser, retrieving soft leather cuffs and a blindfold. Tonight, he was in no hurry. Tonight was for both of them—for unwinding, for surrender, for the exquisite balance of power and trust.

He secured her wrists to the headboard, the leather snug but gentle against her skin. The blindfold came next, plunging her into darkness and amplifying every other sense. Anderson stood back for a moment, taking in the sight of her—bound, blindfolded, and waiting for him with perfect patience.

"You've been a good girl today," he said, his voice low and deliberate. "But tonight, I want to see just how good you can be."

The first touch was feather-light, his fingers grazing her spine in a teasing trail that made her shiver. He smiled at her response, retrieving a slim paddle from the bedside table. The cool wood kissed her skin before he drew it back.

The first strike was gentle, a playful tap that coaxed a sharp exhale from her lips. He continued, alternating between soft, teasing strokes and firmer ones, the sound of impact blending with her breathy moans. Between each strike, his hand soothed her skin, grounding her, reminding her that she was safe.

"You take this so beautifully," he murmured, his voice thick with approval. "Do you like it when I push you?"

"Yes, Sir," she gasped, her body arching instinctively toward him.

He chuckled, setting the paddle aside in favor of his palm. The strikes came faster now, sharper, the sharp crack of his hand meeting her skin filling the room. Clare's moans deepened, her body surrendering to the rhythm of his touch.

But Anderson wasn't done. A silk scarf trailed across her back, a sensual counterpoint to the heat of his strikes. Then came the icy kiss of a cube against her reddened skin, making her gasp and writhe. He kept her teetering on the edge, a masterpiece of contrasts, each sensation drawing her deeper into his control.

When he finally released her wrists and removed the blindfold, she collapsed into his arms, trembling but glowing with satisfaction. Anderson held her close, stroking her hair, murmuring words of praise that made her melt further into him.

"You were perfect," he said, his voice full of warmth and pride.

"Thank you, Sir," she replied, her voice soft but radiant with gratitude.

Anderson kissed her forehead, his exhaustion melting away in the glow of her contentment. This—*she*—was why he pushed so hard, why he endured the chaos of the outside world. Clare was his sanctuary, his solace, and in this moment, nothing else mattered. Together, they were untouchable.

About the Author

Clare

By day, Clare navigates the high-stakes, fast-paced world of IT as a Project Manager, juggling timelines, managing people, and taming chaos with a sharp mind and relentless precision. She's the one you want in the trenches when everything's on fire—methodical, unflappable, and always five steps ahead. But when the workday ends, Clare trades the demands of leadership for a far more personal kind of surrender.

For Clare, BDSM isn't just about submission; it's about trust, vulnerability, and the exhilarating freedom of letting go. Her introduction to the lifestyle began quietly—a whisper of curiosity, a flicker of "what if?"—and quickly grew into a defining part of her identity. In a life filled with decisions, responsibilities, and endless problem-solving, submission offers her the rare gift of existing completely in the moment, safe in the knowledge that Anderson is there to catch her.

What Clare loves most is the creativity. The same meticulous planning that makes her unstoppable at work translates beautifully into their scenes. But here, the stakes are different: it's about building trust, testing boundaries, and finding joy in every shiver, sigh, and spark. Whether she's kneeling in anticipation of Anderson's arrival or diving headfirst into a daring new experience, Clare thrives on the push-and-pull of their dynamic. Outside the playroom, she's a lover of psychology and storytelling, bringing an insatiable curiosity about human nature into their shared adventures.

Anderson

Anderson spends his days at the helm of digital strategy as a Senior Executive, making high-pressure decisions and steering complex projects toward success. It's a world of tight deadlines, endless meetings, and unrelenting expectations, where precision and control are non-negotiable. But when the workday ends, Anderson leaves the sharp edges of the corporate battlefield behind and steps into a role where control takes on a deeper, more intimate meaning.

For Anderson, dominance isn't about power for power's sake. It's about connection, care, and the profound satisfaction of crafting experiences that leave both him and Clare utterly fulfilled. BDSM is his sanctuary, a way to unwind from the chaos of the outside world while deepening his bond with the woman who anchors him.

He cherishes the moments when Clare surrenders—not from fear, but from trust. That trust is the foundation of everything he does, the driving force behind every command, every caress, every carefully planned scene. Anderson approaches dominance with the same thoughtfulness that makes him a leader in his professional life. He plans with precision, always putting Clare's safety and well-being first, but he thrives on adaptability, reading her reactions in the moment and shifting course when needed.

Outside the bedroom, Anderson is a thinker, fascinated by the intersections of control, freedom, and human connection. For him, BDSM is art, a way to transform the mundane into the extraordinary. Every scene is a story, and he takes pride in guiding Clare through every page of it.

Together – A Love Story with Kink at Its Core

Clare and Anderson are more than partners in BDSM; they are partners in life. Their shared passion for exploring the boundaries of trust, creativity, and pleasure has deepened their connection in ways neither of them imagined when they first began this journey. For them, BDSM isn't just a practice; it's woven into the fabric of their relationship, a language that speaks to their souls.

What sets their dynamic apart is the balance they've cultivated. Clare's natural curiosity and willingness to embrace vulnerability perfectly complement Anderson's confidence and care as a Dominant. Together, they create a symphony of scenes, from playful and mischievous to deeply intense, always surprising and delighting each other.

When Anderson comes home after a grueling day, Clare knows exactly how to ground him: a kneeling posture, a flicker of mischief in her eye, and the quiet, undeniable promise that tonight will belong to them. And when Clare's world feels like it's spinning out of control, Anderson is her steady hand, bringing her back to herself with firm words, gentle touches, and the unwavering presence that makes her feel safe.

They wrote this book not as experts preaching from on high, but as a couple who have stumbled, learned, and thrived together. They've made mistakes, pushed limits, and discovered just how far trust and passion can take a relationship. This book isn't a blueprint; it's an invitation to explore your own journey, to take what resonates and make it your own.

Clare and Anderson are living proof that BDSM isn't about fitting into a mold. It's about discovering what makes your relationship flourish, celebrating every moment, and crafting a story that's uniquely yours. For them, the lifestyle isn't just about dominance and submission—it's about love, trust, and the unbridled joy of finding freedom in surrender and control.

www.ingramcontent.com/pod-product-compliance
Lightning Source LLC
Chambersburg PA
CBHW072210070526
44585CB00015B/1278